Highlights of Hinduism

The Path for Peace, Progress & Prosperity

"वसुधैव कुटुम्बकम् ।" (Rig Veda)

The world is but one family.

Highlights of HINDUISM

(The Path for Peace, Progress & Prosperity)

M. Ramakrishna Rao

In Association with

VIDYA BOOKS

SERIALS PUBLICATIONS

NEW DELHI (INDIA)

First Published - 2010

ISBN: 978-81-8387-416-8

Published by

SERIALS PUBLICATIONS
4830/24, Prahlad Street, Ansari Road
Darya Ganj, New Delhi-110002 (India)
Phone : 23245225 Fax : 91-11-23272135
E-mail: serials@satyam.net.in

**THE BENIGN GOLDEN THRONE
OF WORLD POWER**

Meditation should have a base with a meaning and purpose. Of all the representations of divinity in spiritual exercises the above picture of Sri Ram has great significance. Concentrating on it for a few moments elivates consciousness mystically. It symbolises Ramarajyam, kingdom of god, sublimating the supreme power which governs the seen and unseen world. Ram represents the best of humans and celestials for all ages. Many great Muslim, Christian and other spiritual scholars lavished their praise on SRI RAM for his character and inumerable universally adorable qualities. Mature reason gives rise to faith. You can experience the soul-awakening and blissful feeling of peace.

In the begining of our society, every homestead was virtually a RAM MANDIR when Ram ruled the world. People lived happily with good health and prosperity everywhere. We can bring back this glorious social state of Ramarajyam and make this world a kingdom of GOD again. To begin with we have choosen Visakhapatnam to translate our ideas into action (even as the sun rises in this Eastren city to spread its rays far and wide.)

** For details please write to the Author with your full address*

To

My Parents

Contents

Foreword

Highlights of Hinduism is a pleasurable compendium of the best thoughts on the subject. The sweep of this book is breath-taking, from the most ancient Vedic time to the futuristic society of the 21st Century. An incisive analysis of the varied concepts of religion and spirituality is presented with consummate skill. One finds quotations from almost all the scriptures including the Vedas, Gita, Upanishads, the Bible, the Koran and all the founders of religious thought besides social philosophers from Voltaire to Bertrand Russell and a host of authorities. Gandhian philosophy is specially highlighted by devoting to it a whole chapter in the book. The analysis of concepts of happiness, Knowledge, duty, liberation, mysticism, Yoga, Human Resources Development (HRD) and many related theories is illuminating and the reader is led into an ecstatic world of spiritual experience. Solutions can be found for the whole gamut of social problems by assimilating and practising the values and norms expounded in the several chapters under the significant sub-headings. The Author conceives 21st Century as one of Peace and propounded the idea of observing a Peace-Fortnight from the 1st to 15th of January each year. His plea for banning Boxing as a sport in the civilized world is also relevant in this context. The principles of Globalization and Liberalization are emphasized by the Author to obliterate "the barriers built by history and wars" and to make every person feel the joy of human birth. Even a casual reader is bound to experience a feeling of expansiveness and happiness while a serious study of the book clears many doubts regarding the relevance and application of religious thought in modern life. To quote John Milton, *"Many a man lives a burden to the earth; but a good book is the precious life-blood of a Master spirit"*. It is rarely that we come across the work of a genius. Mankind is indeed blessed to have a remarkable exposition of Hinduism as a Universal Religion fit to be practised by all human beings in the modern world.

G.J. NEHRU
Rosy Apartments,
Gopalapuram, Madras.

Acknowledgement

I am happy that ***Shri Ramachandran Nayar of Vidya*** **Books** had readily taken up the task of publishing my different essays in a compendious book form with high standards befitting the subject and the title "Highlights of Hinduism". I am greatly indebted to Shri C.S.S. Menon who edited the wide-ranging material and ideas expressed by me on the different subjects, with great devotion and understanding. We rarely come across such enthusiasm and dedication to a noble cause. The manuscripts have been scrutinized and compared carefully with the proofs from time to time with utmost concern for the quality of the book. I may also record my thankfullness to my wife, Smt. Ramadevi B.A., for reading out the proofs to me. My gratitude is also due to the many scholars with whom I interacted over the years.

M. Ramakrishan Rao

Publisher's Note

Why is our country still poor despite our acclaimed resources of men and materials?! The hope for India lies in the true spiritual awakening of our people, different from what is being done all these years, by comprehending the Vedic ideals properly. To serve the true Vedic Religion of Hinduism and make it UNIVERSAL WITH A MODERN SCIENTIFIC OUTLOOK, a dedicated work was undertaken by the author during the last five decades. The result is an authentic and stimulating exposition of Hinduism for the layman as also the scholar. When the fate of India is in the balance as it were, we should tilt the scales in our favour by proper understanding of our duties and goals. Thus, this Book serves the noblest of all causes.

Preface

A deep study of the present day Indian society in its entirety and the processes of development through the last 62 years after Independence reveals that we can still build up a glorious future for our people and also contribute to human progress all over the world in the spirit of a global family. We should take immediate stock of the situation and implement wholesome measures on a warfooting throughout the country. They must be in keeping with the noble heritage of spiritual and ethical values based on the ancient lore as also the modern thought on scientific lines. The law of love is supreme in this context. This brings peace within and without, which can be experienced. Educated people should try to keenly think about this. Vain repetitions of what is stated in books, past or present, will not help. *To think is to pray and to work is to worship.* There is an inherent and perennial spring of goodness and happiness in every being which has to be harnessed. In that process some harsh words may have to be employed though with great humility and affection as Gandhiji himself had stated to have done. (Collected works Vol. 20-p.507). I penned down this treatise **in obedience to the injunction of Taittiriya and Kenopanishads that the spiritual truth should not only be experienced but also spread in society.**

Steeped in vain-glorious ideas of greatness of Indian heritage and Hinduism, it is very hard for us to accept any criticism how-soever well-founded or authentic it may be. This is the unfortunate euphoria created by the catena of teachers, priests and writers throughout our history, ancient and modern. It is difficult to explain as to how they have missed or overlooked the vital aspects or the very life-force of Hinduism based on Vedanta. It may not be an exaggeration to say that our so-called philosophers lived in a "fools' paradise" and lead the whole nation into believing that to be the El Dorado. Real Hinduism was synonymous with Ram rajya.

In the name of Hinduism all that the scholars have been doing through writings and speeches is mere repetition of statements, stories and quotations from the scriptures, epics and commentaries in a pedantic way giving their own whimsical interpretations. Simple truths propounded in the Veda, Upanishads and Gita have been complicated and distorted in the plethora of publications, old and new, by all and sundry. Personalised cults, societies, ashrams and institutions, big and small, have dug inroads into the healthy growth of spiritual wisdom of universal purport true to our Vedantic foundation. Very few have given any serious thought to save the people from the strangle-hold of the superstitions, blind religious practices, irrational and wasteful rituals etc. which like parasites drain away the wealth and mental health of the people. They only repeated parrot-like, passages from the available literature, working out some permutations and combinations. This justified the parasitical existence of a section of people without any contribution to the growth of our society in real terms. All the confused religious teachers and swamis to this day simply chant as a miraculous Mantra the negative idea of giving up attachment to action and wealth.

Highly talented persons are also mislead by the constant outpourings of our religious teachers of all shades and descriptions demanding detachment, inaction, passivity etc. as a panacea for all ills whereas tireless productive work is the true norm.

The Symbolism developed in our ancient lore has not been properly understood. We have misinterpreted and misapplied the treasures of the philosophic and spiritual foundation laid by the Rishis and Sages. Even in the face of mind-boggling developments in space programmes, biotechnology, lasers, robotics, limb transplants, OHS, Super computers etc. people indulge in ridiculous religious practices without true spiritual purport or sanction. The youth of the country have to bear the brunt of poverty, overpopulation, disease and sufferings inflicted on the people by lack of will to reform the existing systems in the name of tradition. This is applicable to all faiths having a free-play and commanding spheres of influence over the gullible people to serve some vested interests inimical to social growth.

Hinduism gives the highest value to knowledge or the mind which is synonymous with it. This is the milk of life. Taking the world metaphorically as water, imagine the situation where only a little milk is thrown into a lake of water. This is the decadence. To give another example, the mind, as a boat, floats in the water of the world, but the boat cannot float without the water and the bigger it is, the larger shall be the area of water. Imagine a stagnant pool with a concourse of paper boats therein. The most striking norm for good life has been spelt out to be one of service to others and to society. *'Paropakaram' 'Manava Seva'* i.e., helping others and service to mankind are the two values. It is enjoined that every effort should be made to create wealth which is conducive to the happiness of man. Self-realisation has been given importance in order to pepare the human-being to face life with fortitude and find joy in the pursuit of perfection.

Sages Vasishta and Viswamitra were great teachers who guided Lord Rama. Lack of such teachers created doubts and confusion in the minds of the great Buddha, Mahaveera and others who relinquished their wordly duties and subjected themselves to self-torture, for the sake of mankind. Righteous action and not giving up desires is the foundation for growth. Life is not evil as taught wrongly in some religious quarters but a celebration and a means for higher life. This was the Vedic and Vedantic exhortation. "Cast all your burdens on the Lord" is a catchy shibboleth capitalised by the priests, pandits, mullas etc. whereas ceaseless endeavour for creating wealth and improving the quality of life, utilizing our faculties to the utmost is the norm prescribed by the sages of yore as I have understood from my authentic studies of all the scriptures and lives of the truly great souls of whom lord Rama in the ancient world and Mahatma Gandhi in the present world are outstanding.

If there is some good in the work that was done in earlier times pursuant to sincere efforts to translate the noble tenets of Hinduism into action, it is only rudimentary. The case for *Jantar-Mantar* in New Delhi as an observatory cannot be matched against the high-technology-supported astronomical research of the Western World. Lasers, Molecular Biology, Nuclear Physics, Radio-telescopes, space probes and many such unimaginable developments could be achieved by the scientists in the world when we were counting only the nine planets (including the imaginary Rahu and Ketu) and circumambulating the Nava Graha images in the temples.

It is a near comical situation as we keep on singing the praise of our Motherland as full of sweet water, fruits, food, cool air etc. and at the same time allow drought, famine, disease, pollution and other evils to stalk the land. In a premier city which is acclaimed as a cultural capital of India, water taps are dry for most part of the day and slums are everywhere. Blind or thoughtless praise without proper understanding can also damage the image in another sense. Mr. Nani A. Palkhivala in his booklet 'India's priceless heritage', which already ran into six editions, published by Bharatiya Vidya Bhavan opens the chapter "Mother India" with this observation- "It has been my long-standing conviction that India is like a donkey carrying a sack of gold". The general editors late Shri R.R. Diwakar and Shri S. Ramakrishnan as also Swami Ranganathananda who wrote the foreword have acquiesced in such a misconceived and demeaning statement. To say the least, it is in very bad taste. Similarly, Dr. S. Gopal chose to write the biography of his illustrious father and former president of India Dr. S. Radhakrishnan, who was acclaimed for his knowledge of Hindu Philosophy, but wrote in the very first para of the book (published by the reputed Oxford Publications) about the doubtful legitimacy of Dr. Radhakrishnan's birth basing it on surmises. This is a great blow to the image of a venerable personality, particularly, when he is not there to refute it. I knew Dr. Radhakrishnan as an affectionate and lofty-minded person and spent many hours with him on several occasions in private conversation. A progressive thinker and Head of the State deserved more consideration.

Multiplying the rituals and paraphernalia which are resulting in clumsiness and unhygienic practices should be scrupulously avoided. The spiritual significance of Religious events has to be understood and propagated, which will mitigate blind superstitious practices. For example, in 1992, lakhs of people converged in Kumbakonam and entered the Mahamaham Tank with insufficient water, resulting in a stampede and virtual bloodbath. The much publicized myth or story of some nectar having fallen into the tank ages ago was the cause for all this. The Pushkarams or once-in-12 years festivals of ablution in Ganga, Godavari, Krishna and other flowing rivers are different. We should pause and analyse the pros and cons of certain religious beliefs in the modern context. Blindly following some old religious institutions has only added to the idleness, waste and other evils which can be avoided by deeper study and true spiritual understanding. It is my sincere attempt to promote this new awareness, based on authentic studies of the scriptural texts and classics in the spiritual field, followed by rigorous Yogic practices.

If we carefully analyse the facts, most of the preachers took to philosophy not by choice but merely by chance or as an escape or out of helplessness, which resulted in large-scale distortion and predominance of personal vagaries. Their false humility is also misleading. Beyond earning a livelihood or fulfilling family and social obligations we owe a duty to ourselves for spiritual upliftment to experience the true joy of human birth. There is no need to run away from worldly responsibilities, leaving dependants in the lurch or causing anguish to 'near and dear'. Ironically many religious leaders have adopted this extreme path. Raghavendra Swami (1624-71) was very poor and brought up by his brother-in-law when he lost his parents. He married Saraswathi and begot a son. He took to Sanyasa all on a sudden, pursuant to a dream even without telling his wife. She lost hope and out of despair jumped into a well and died. His biography "Raghavendra Vijaya" by his sister's son Narayanachar gives an account of the life and miracles. Swami Sivananda was also reported to have left his family abruptly to settle down in Rishikesh. Aurobindo Ghosh ran away from Calcutta leaving his wife in a pitiable plight, to settle down in Pondicherry. Many unbelievable stories of runaways and dropouts becoming religious leaders make one sad to reflect on the unfortunate conditions of their own life and their families. No doubt they were great sons of our Motherland who took to their varied missions in a spirit of utmost sacrifice. I invoked their pardon, indulgence and blessings for the critical views I have expressed in this essay.

It was enjoined in the Sastras that one should not take to Sanyasa without the free consent of the wife. Otherwise, it tantamounts to violence to Dharmik life. Spirituality cannot result from a sinful life. The gullibility and generosity of people made mountains of molehills and vested interests took over to exploit the religious sentiments. Further, there are many stories of Swamis and Babas losing temper and acting funnily on occasions. That betrays their immaturity, unsteadiness, inferiority complex and sense of insecurity. Vested interests interpreted the eccentricities and ignorant ways of the Babas, as prompted by 'Divine will' and read meanings to suit the propaganda requirements. Another disconcerting tendency in modern times is the institutionalization to perpetuate the narrow cults and creeds where the founders are magnified as more than Gods under wrong notions of Guruhood.

The role of a teacher is purely personal and cannot be passed on as an office of profit. Institutionalization has also done great damage to the purity where successors are chosen on irrelevant considerations. Ineptitude characterizes most of these institutions and the administrative heads, which is resulting in disharmony and disaffection in the society. I have spared no efforts and left no stones unturned to get at the real world of spirituality. I have visited almost all the institutions and met the religious heads and find that there is great scope for improving their outlook and integrating the rivulets of good religious thought into a great magnanimous reservoir of spirituality for the benefit of mankind.

Therefore, it is our responsibility to analyse the concepts dinned into our ears by the misguided philosophers, ignorant swamis, blabbering Babas, self-centred priests and others when we may reject the whole lot as gibberish, not conducive to real growth. A great sense of discipline and purposefulness guided the Western countries to progress towards high living standards for their people. We have to open our eyes to the realities of the world and realize the harm that has resulted from the emphasis given to the negative principles of our philosophy by the whole lot of thinkers, ancient and modern. **Our society has been smoking away for ages without seeing the real light of prosperity for the people with all our acclaimed resources of men and materials.** We have now to start afresh with a new understanding and determination in a spirit of 'now or never, do or die!'

We have to launch a vigorous campaign of social work by all the religious institutions, societies etc. in India, harnessing the men, materials and other properties available with them instead of confining their activities to self-perpetuation with a dog-in-the-manger attitude. We should dissolve the cult affiliations and swear only by national interest. Education, vocational training centres, farm activities, public hygiene, medical attention and such other activities should be given top priority for being activated by these religious institutions of all shades and descriptions, big and small, all over the country. Then only the real impact for positive growth will be realized which is the true spirit or ideal of all religions and particularly of Hinduism. I have attempted to put the matters in the right perspective after assimilating the essence of Hinduism through years of unremitting labour of love involving the body, mind and heart (*Drishti, Sravana, Manana and Nidhidhyasa*). The pseudo-secular atmosphere and the resultant apathy or ignorance of the educated people regarding the true merits of Hinduism can be suicidal to our society. The dying fires of right knowledge and spirituality have to be rekindled without further loss of time. This is my humble prayer and lifelong effort.

M. RAMAKRISHNA RAO

1

Introduction

Hinduism has the highest objective of eliminating evil and suffering in the world as declared in the earliest of its scriptures Rigveda (*Apaghnanto Ravnah*). It balances the worldly (*Aihika*) with the spiritual (*Amushmika*). It enjoins efforts for achieving prosperity and happiness (*Sivan ... Abhivajan*). The Rishis gave expression to their perceptions from the highest plane of consciousness (*Paramevyoman*). This knowledge should be spread to all the people (*Avadani Jana Anu*). Co-operative endeavour for progress was prescribed. The king or ruler was elected by the people (*Visona Rajanam Vrumah*). Idleness and Selfishness are condemned (*Kevalagho Bhavati Kevaladi*). Divinity manifests through matter and unity is achieved amongst the people by spirituality. The Vedic literature has poetical excellence with special structures or prosody. God is conceived as permeating the entire creation and is not limited by the existence of an anti-God of Satan. The concept defies categorization by likeness, relationship, numbers, sex, age, size etc. It is thus individualized according to one's comprehension, liking and development. It includes all and excludes none. This Catholicity or universality is sustained throughout in the Vedic literature. This was truly experienced by the Rishis and is different from the 'opinions' of the scholars. While I can quote innumerable examples for this unity of experience in the diversity of opinions I content myself with giving a typical passage from Yajur Veda which lays down the profoundest experience of the Rishis *"Vedahametam Purusham Mahantam, Aditya Varnam.. Nanyah Pantha Vidyate..."*. Briefly stated, it means "I have experienced the supreme...there is no other way for this...". (*Y. Vajasaneyi Samhita*). The vision of the divinity in creation is repeatedly presented in the Vedic literature. Creativity is given the highest value. The Supreme Creator is described as the poet of poets – *"Kavim Kavinam"*. If we are true to the spirit of the Vedic religion we will be able to get over many of the obstacles created by the confused interpretations and idle theories expounded by self-centred preachers, priests, scholars, swamis and others who did not have proper grinding in the original texts or spiritual exposure. I have sincerely attempted to recapture the excellence of Hinduism in these highlights, minimizing the exuberance of unnecessary details.

In ancient times people lived in awe and fear of the forces of nature which were uncontrollable and caused misery to their lives. In due course, they learnt to protect themselves and harness nature to serve their needs and enhance the comforts of life. In the process they became very meticulous and attached sanctity to every conceivable activity including the routine things like eating, sleeping etc., which are of no consequence to the common man. Some strange perceptions were developed. The priest class almost went wild with their imagination and created a whole body of rituals, chantings etc. which provided some thrill. Unfortunately, the important elements in Hindu Philosophy have been camouflaged or missed by the majority of the so-called philosophers and thinkers throughout our history. They only repeated the available literature, working out some permutations and combinations. This justified the parasitical existence of a section of people without any contribution to the growth of our society in real terms.

Many so-called religious and spiritual leaders didn't have proper lives or study and care during their childhood days. The Western educated scholars had no grinding in the classical texts or spiritual exposure. They both are thus poles apart missing the essential requirement for spiritual understanding of life.

The promotion of Ahimsa was the main role of Jainism which is represented by the 24 *Theerthankars* of whom Mahaveera is well-known. It is told that the first Theerthankar was Vrishabhanatha, a king with Ayodya as his capital. He had hundred sons by his first wife of whom Bharata was the eldest. Bahubali or Gomateswara whose statues have been erected in recent times was the only son of the second wife, Sunanda Devi. A big battle ensued between the two sons, but after victory, Bahubali retired to the forests to perform Thapas for "Kevala Jnana" which is the ultimate attainment. This is very near to the story of Mahabharat with Dhritarashtra having a hundred sons and war being fought between members of the family. However, no statues have been built for the victors. Mahaveera also fought a battle with his brother and after vanquishing him, retired to forest for *Thapas* in the same way as the first *Theerthankara*. We have to sift the material and stories to arrive at the practicable principles of *Ahimsa* in the present times. Lord Buddha who was almost a contemporary of Mahaveera, did not have to fight any battle, but sacrified his kingdom and the pleasures of the royalty. Both of them subjected themselves to self-torture of unimaginable severity for the sake of mankind. As their thoughts were limited to the worldly existence and suffering, they could not satisfy the spiritual aspirations and other-worldly ideas nurtured by the Vedic lore. It is also worth mentioning that both of them did not have spiritual teachers usually associated with royal houses (like Vasishta and Viswamitra in the case of Rama) with the result that they sought spiritual solutions on their own without any serious study or guidance provided by Gurus. They relinquished their worldly duties and taught the extreme principles of giving up desires. The principle of Ahimsa was also taken to the logical extreme with practices like covering the nose and mouth with a peace of cloth, eating food before night-fall, abstaining from worldly activities etc. If Hinduism and its off-shoots, Buddhism and Jainism are deeply analysed, *righteous action and not giving up desires is the real foundation for growth.* There cannot be life at all without worldly desires which can be sublimated by ideals.

Real love for Motherland should be shown in constructive work in whatever humble way possible and not merely in words or voluminous verbiage as indulged in by most of our modern philosophers and leaders.

The Rishis did everything for the establishment of peace and all their utterances conclude with a note and prayer for peace of the world. In such a land, we are finding violence on an unprecedented scale. We have to analyse the reasons and rectify our methods of working. The educated people have a great role to play apart from the policy-makers. The scenes in the parliament where members lose their tempers should open our eyes to the need of educating them. The TV, Radio, Newspapers, Magazines, Films etc. project violence and crime in different degrees. The Vedic Rishis have exhorted the educated to play their role properly for building up a good and peaceful society (*Swadhyaya Pravachana*). Gandhiji had branded all those who fail in their duty to promote the above social values as "Educated Rascals".

After much study and contemplation I could arrive at the definition of the word 'Hindu' to answer the new role true to the noble tenets as laid down by the Rishis and Sages of Yore. *"Hinam Dushayati Va Durayati iti Hindu"*, i.e. a person who discourages evil and helps in its atonement. *If this definition is adopted, a Hindu will have universal acceptance once again as in the Vedic age.*

The Hindu ethos can be said to have been developed in and around temples as centres for growth-oriented programmes with the under-current of spirituality. The structures, buildings, lands, and other properties endowed for the temples have to be harnessed suitably in the modern context benefiting the individual, family, group and the society at large. Professionalisation and not commercialisation should be the theme. Behaviour, attitude and skills can be influenced, upgraded and modernized. Income-generating programmes can be conceived in culture related areas. Some of the social problems can also be identified and solved, anticipated and prevented. The strength to withstand suffering, determination to work for betterment, creating healthy and peaceful environment, urge to improve knowledge levels and such personal and social values will take root in the minds of the people. Multiplying the rituals and paraphernalia promoting clumsiness and unhygienic practices should be scrupulously avoided. The spiritual significance has to be understood and propagated which will mitigate blind superstitious practices.

Self-esteem should be differentiated from egoism or vanity. **Positive thinking is the bedrock of Hinduism.** Despondency is to be avoided. Prayer restores composure and builds up the above qualities. A sense of wonder at the rich endowments in nature and human physiology imparts commitment and thankfulness. Karma theory or belief in destiny is an antidote for grumbling mentality. Cheerfulness is a sign of spiritual learning. Respect for human dignity is the result of true awakening. Anger is a sign of immaturity in man. Service to the society is the only urge for a self-realised soul. All faculties, facilities, learning, expertise, skills and activities should be directed to subserve the above cause. Loka Sangraham or welfare of the society is the only purpose and end of righteous action. This is the highest goal set for man. The purpose of this book is to highlight the fact that all the important principles which form the core of Hinduism spell out the objective of welfare of mankind as one large family. In that sense, Hinduism should be accepted as a truly universal religion cutting across all barriers of language, colour, creed, State and Nationality.

The strength of Hinduism really lies in the fact that it lays stress on work according to one's station in life. Faith in God works as a Catalyst. "All things work together for good to them that love God" (Bible). For an Avatar to descend on the earth evil should keep on growing as per our existing belief which may not be an acceptable proposition. At any rate, an Avatar may kill an invincible and incorrigible evil-doer but the purpose of saints is to remove the evil in man. I believe that this saintliness can be developed in ourselves by self-analysis and determination to do good. In simple words, refraining from doing harm by words or deeds to fellow human beings is the easiest way to be good. The better way is to sacrifice a little of what we have for the good of others. Is it not a pity that we should depend on the munificence of foreigners to promote our spiritual activities and well-being? In psychology they say "When people know what they are expected to be they tend to identify themselves with that description". The quackery, pseudo-science, archaic beliefs, outdated and irrelevant charlatanism in the form of astrology, rituals and other religious mumbo-jumbo promoted by the ashrams, societies etc., for their survival should be shunned in the interest of the growth of a vibrant and progressive society as conceived by our forbears and the Founding-Fathers of our Constitution.

I have passed through a wonderful range of mystical experiences from my childhood including conversing with Gods and Goddesses in a physical plane, going into a trance or Samadhi state, reaching super-conscious or intuitive levels of thinking, miraculously escaping from dangers, premonition of events, cognition of incomprehensible truths and many more things of the widest range possible from the trivial to the most magnificent. A glance through my book of poems "THE PEARLS FROM DEVOTION" will easily convince any reasonable person of the truth of my above statement. In fact I penned down most of the poems in a state of super-consciousness or communion with the divine. Though I studied the best literary works in English, Sanskrit and Telugu and the techniques of poetical writing or prosody intensely, I hardly imagined that divine poetry could flow so spontaneously out of my pen till I saw it in black & white and acclaimed by the scholars who read it. It was a matter of self-fulfilment for me. The joy in such an experience can be reaped by all if they can reach the fountain of the heart through their own work in dedication to God. This is the highest note of the Hindu philosophy.

Hinduism gives utmost importance to women, children and youth in that order. In fact the very Goddesses of wisdom and wealth, viz. Saraswathi and Lakshmi bear out the truth of this phenomenon. They are the very foundation for a happy home. All the others are secondary. The belief in some quarters that wisdom and wealth are mutually exclusive is a total misconception. They are complementary and provide the balance in life. Some ignorant writers have depicted them to be at loggerheads and it caught on the imagination of people generally. We have to uproot such superstitious thinking and promote respect for learning and dedication to duty as visible representations of the two Goddesses for the integrated and healthy growth of the society.

The mother is credited with the mental make-up of the child. She implants the seed of motivation and meaningful employment of energies. The widely popular morning prayer in India of Lord Venkateswara starts with the words "*Kousalya Supraja Rama ,,,,,,,,,* "meaning - "O Rama, worthy son of Kousalya! awake and take up the work for the day". Mostly our prayers are mere notional praise or catalogue of names. Instead they should spell out national commitment and work-culture. Children are also burdened with huge loads of books which they carry to schools on bent backs. It is a pitiable sight. We should preserve the potential and the tender feelings in them. Life should not be made burdensome even at that age. The tender sprout is given freedom to grow and it can bear the burdens when fully grown. This is the nature's law of growth. Long treatises on the subjects are also self-defeating. Too many subjects should not be introduced in children's education curriculum, which dissipate their mental caliber.

The energy of the youth is the life-blood of the Nation. Frustration and disenchantment with our systems should not be allowed to cripple their outlook. If we properly present the basics of our philosophy to them in their formative years there will be no scope for destructive propensities, abstention from work and violence of every kind that is in evidence nowadays. We should propagate relentlessly the value of time and the need to utilize every moment of our life in productive enterprise and in creativity to herald a new era of peace and progress. Unfortunately, self-realisation, Nirvana and other ideals have been presented in a totally wrong perspective throughout the life of our Nation. China was mislead by the ideas borrowed from us into their Taoism with such norms-"if the man is divested of all his sense perception, this is the goal". They took to the "Nasal Gaze" or looking at the tip of one's nose as a Yogic practice for *Nirvana*. Thus, several of the Hindu beliefs percolated to the different countries in the Far East also. Later on, many were converted by the Arabs with their peculiar morals of killing people, having four wives etc. The Chinese revolution wiped out the idleness from their society as also, unfortunately, the interest in spiritual pursuits. The Japanese have virtually made a somersault towards progress. We have to take a lesson from the happenings in these two countries and prepare our youth for the new challenges of work and new philosophy of peace. The vast mass of literature which goes under the banner of religion and philosophy in India is devoid of merit by propagating idleness and meaningless activities catering to the demands of ego and the creeds. I have seen the idle way people sit in supposed contemplation in ashrams, societies etc. under the (mis) guidance of ill-informed and selfish spiritual pedlars. We have to ban this type of so-called spiritual activity from the land and subject the self-styled teachers of Vedanta to strict work norms. We have to rewrite our philosophy to prohibit the preaching of idleness of any kind, which is different from what Bertrand Russel conceived in his famous (humorous) essay "In praise of idleness". Freedom is great fun not in goosing around quacking about past glories or sitting gloomily contemplating on the next meal but in galloping towards the distant goals set for ourselves in the National Charter!

In olden days they naturally tended to stretch things to occupy the idle time. What takes minutes was dragged into days, days into months, months into years. We should reverse this trend and instill workmindedness and positive approach to life in the people. The religious institutions and all individuals engaged in related activities should be exposed to modern scientific understanding to promote social growth and creation of wealth by giving up their idle ways and preachings. The glorification of poverty should first be removed form our religious thinking. While the wealthy can become wealthier, we can make the healthy healthier and the poor happy by restructuring and revamping our religious institutions with work orientation and new awareness. I have incisively analysed the critical norms of Hinduism in this book and have also presented the absolute need for cultivating a 'Modern mind' in keeping with the spirit of Hinduism.

The Indian Constitution clearly sets out the goals to be achieved, the rights and duties of citizens, directives of State Policy which are fundamental in the governance of the country, independence of the judiciary, responsibilities of the executive, supremacy of Parliament and many details and mechanisms for the realization of the glorious ideals. People should be educated about these values, institutions, systems, procedures etc. It will contribute in no small measure to the material and spiritual well-being of people. It may be noted that the Gayatri Mantra, which is the kingpin of the chantings, is a prayer for the rousing of the higher intellect. Most of the Vedic Mantras are prayers for such endowments for worldly life. While some are concerned with lofty matters like spiritual luster, power, ability, cattle wealth etc. others pray for eyesight, hearing, good teeth etc. Though some mantras have intrinsic word power or spiritual vibration, it is futile to simply repeat the texts and chantings endlessly without understanding the purport. The Vedic Rishi was clearly directing his attention towards worldly action for creating wealth, though in the hazardous and unpredictable nature of his surroundings, the accent was naturally more on appeasing the multifarious Gods and demi-Gds. To give a simple example, even a little amount of ghee cannot be obtained except through the tending of cows, milking them and churning the milk etc. Every step or event in the process is related to some unknown power and prayers are offered for better results. Simply praying for more ghee without doing the work involved would not do! Once knowledge is obtained about the various events, self-confidence increased and systematic efforts have been developed.

The four stages of life called "Ashramas" have been conceived in the context of bringing out the best of life through appropriate work at every stage. Dharma or righteousness permeates all the ashramas as indicated by Manu in his Dharmasastra (Code) "Dharme nasramo karanam". All the Vedic injunctions are predominantly work-oriented and require us to utilize our faculties fully for universal development. This is the spiritual significance or meaning of "Purusha Sukta". Every activity is reflected in the being through the various faculties, limbs and organs forming part of the body. By caring for the well-being and growth of each and every aspect of existence we will build up the healthy and integrated personally of the Homo Sapiens. This is the noble path towards peace for the individual as well as for mankind.

The great sages of ancient India deeply probed into the complexities of life and the reasons for the suffering. Withdrawal from involvement in worldly activities was advisedly an easy solution to avoid the concomitant results. This was termed as "Udaseenata". This is also a type of neutrality which enables a person not to be agitated by the happenings around him. The Gita clearly emphasizes worldly action in preference to inaction (Karmajyayo ....). One should earn his livelihood by righteous action and not by preaching or practising inaction. This is also the essence of the Vedic Mantras and the Upanishads. It is further explained that good action bears beneficial fruits of happiness. The great sages have analysed the wrong psyche of people generally when they declared "People want to enjoy the result of good actions without doing them and do not want the effects of evil actions while constantly doing them!" What is required according to Gita is sincere faith in the heart which is the seat of the Lord. This can be nourished by appropriate readings to educate the mind on true spiritual values. This is the implication of the Yogic idea "Oordhwa Moolam....". Unfortunately, people have lost the habit of reading the original texts and applying their mind to the problems.

After thoroughly studying the Upanishads and Bagavadgita I am convinced that the Vedantic ideas stated therein for our guidance can be restated in very simple terms. The important Upanishads, viz. Isa, Kena, Katha, Prasna, Mundaka, Mandukya, Taittiriya, Chandogya, Brihadaranyaka and Svetesvatara contain simple truths which have been expatiated upon with elaborate commentaries. Similarly, the Gita which is atated to be the essence of the Upanishads (like the milk of the cow) has also been subjected to lengthy complicated dissertations. Religion without reason and philosophy without faith are futile. The relevant notes on which real Hinduism is based relate to (1)Duty, (2) Discipline, (3) Dedication, (4) Devotion and (5) Freedom or Liberation. The Sanskrit words used are Dharma, Niyama, Sraddha, Bhakti and Mukti besides Udyoga, Udyama, Yatna, Paurusham, Dharmaparatva etc. It is time we disbanded all the idle indtitutions and buried the volumes of books produced by the confused minds associated with them in all the languages all over the country. The purity of the originals, like the unpolluted Ganga will have to be re-established. Hinduism has been acclaimed as a scientific religion., Prof. W.D. Brown describes it as "a thoroughly scientific religion" in his book "The superiority of Vedic Religion". Jagad-guru Bharati Krishna Teertha in his"Vedic Mathematics" brings out the wonderful and magical formulae for solving the problems from the Vedic lore. Instead of pursuing the true scientific and mathematical research, germane to our ancient lore, we have been engaging ourselves in the futility of empty philosophic discourses and wasteful religious rigmarole throughout our history. We should reverse his trends and launch a positive philosophy of work for peace and prosperity for the millions of our people. This is the real heritage of Hinduism.

Modern management ideas and techniques derived their strength from the leadership qualities of the persons who can be called the trend setters for growth. In the galaxy of all-time greats as leaders of men, based on deep study of their personalities and achievements in the given circumstances, I find Lord Rama in the ancient world, Jagadguru Adi Sankaracharya in the medieval times and Mahatma Gandhi in the modern world to be outstanding in all the physical, intellectual and spiritual dimensions. Certain aspects of Sankara's Greatness can inspire the present day managements. The first striking note in his famous 'Shatpadi Stotra' indicates 'Vinaya' which can be translated as "humility and respect for learning" as the foundation on which the whole edifice of success can be built (Avinayamapanaya.......). The other fundamental principle which can be highlighted is the 'sense of duty' as depicted by him throughout his life in obedience to the injunction "Dharmo Rakshati Rakshitah". He never swerved from the duty of establishing Dharma in the whole of India for which he was born. He faced all hazards and subjected himself to utmost strain for fulfilling the duty cast on him as a 'Yati'. He set certain goals for himself and found joy in fulfilling them for the benefit of the world. He mastered the Vedantic lore assiduously and integrated the diverse thoughts into an unified and harmonious system of non-dualism. This is single-mindedness of purpose. The 'integral approach' is the greatest contribution of Sankara to the modern thought. Thus, respect for learning and dedication to duty can be said to be the two eyes for the progress of any society and managements should give topmost priority to these two values.

(a) Sankara also provides deep insight into the 'motivation' factor vital for management success. In his "Upadesa Sahasri", he postulated that even a starving person would not relish poison (Khsudhaya Peedyamanopi.....). Sweetness should characterize the fruit of labour. Appreciation and reward should be guaranteed. A minimum assurance or security for employment in life has to be ensured. Hope for improvement can be built on the trust reposed in management. The sweetness of this hope is the true motivation for growth. We have to reverse the deterrent role and criminal attitude of personnel departments. HRD is a positive engagement stimulating growth beyond mere training function. The hostile and fault-finding approach should be totally eschewed. "Maternalistic management" is the norm.

(b) "Self-esteem" is equally important in the scheme of optimizing productivity. Sankara is so eloquent on this principle throughout his works (Sivoham, Sivoham....), It should be differentiated from false ego or vanity. It is not at all incompatible with discipline or subordination, Far from that. Respect for human dignity should inform all institutions.

(c) 'An analytical mind' is a great asset to an organization. Sankara's "Viveka Choodamani" is replete with ideas relevant to the theme. His commentary on Brahma Sutras also bears the torch for his approach. The very first step he indicates is overwhelming "Ushmadasmad Pratyaya Gocharayoh....". Thus we should differentiate between individual aspirations and corporate goals in the field of management. "They should not work at cross purposes. A "Sense of belonging" should be instilled into the members of the organization. The frequent utterance in corporate circles "We are like a family" should be realized by one and all in the practical working.

(d) 'Idealism' should not be discouraged as impracticable. In fact many great developments were thought to be impossible when conceived! Sankara exhorts people to have high ideals supported by professional knowledge and skills. Then it will not be a case of misguided men behind guided-missiles! In fact there won't be need for missiles at all.

(e) Faith in the Supreme is a catalyst for success. Sankara underlines the 'importance of faith' (Bhaja Govindam ....). It is not to be misunderstood as helplessness leading to self-surrender. We have come across several cases of serendipity in the world of science. But it should not be forgotten that so much preparation should precede before a result can be expected. Sankara's life illustrates the above principle in abundance. He never took chances. He made stupendous preparations which fructified by his own

Yoga. Pathanjali in his "Yoga Sutra" defines it as 'Pratibha' which provides the base and leads on to fulfilment. This is also similar to synergy in modern parlance. To give another example, after a minimum base is created like imparting the required revolutions to the propeller, the aircraft gets lifted into the air. Sankara repeatedly insists on human effort which is the basic norm for good management. Faith in the Supreme and faith in one's own self are the two sides of the coin of success.

(f) Last but not the least, we should place more reliance on the 'enterprise of the youth', than the sedate working methods of the old. We are bogged down by tradition and the conservative approach of the earlier generations. Sankara had revolutionalised the thinking and invigorated the stagnant society with his youthfulness and radiance. This should permeate the management atmosphere in our country. As per the report of RBI more than 50% of sickness in the multitude of industries is due to management deficiency. Most of them are in the hands of people without vision and dynamism. Sankara gave the answer to this malaise. After studying his works in original I am convinced that we should be guided by the above principles embedded in Sankara's philosophy which is the beacon light for 'progress and social growth' which are the ultimate objective in a macro perception for even a micro organization with a sensitive 'Management by Objectives'.

I take this opportunity to present a new management technique based on Sankara's achievement in the successful implementation of his 'Project Indian Spiritual Renaissance'. It can be called "STOCK" as an acronym for strengths, threats, opportunities, Conscience Keepers (similar to the modern management rule of SWOT analysis). Sankara studied all the above mentioned aspects and established the Mutts in select places for servicing the Cause of Dharma. We may import the

"STOCK" methodology beneficially into modern management practices. The 'Highlights of Hinduism' will be serving the cause of man in the spiritual and material dimensions, for the happiness of human beings and good of the society, if on reading the book, the 'Conscience Destroyers' are converted into 'Conscience Keepers' even in a small measure! Others who know can, of course, expect to get a glimpse of the 'unknown'!

The names of the Vedic Rishis are not really known except a few like Angeerasa, Bharadwaja, Vajasraasa, Kanwa, Yavatsara, Kashyapa, Nidhruva who are mentioned in the mantras as part of the text. We find some more names in the Upanishads. In Veda, Gods like Brahma, Agni, Indra, Saraswati, Vishnu, Chandra, Yama, Surya and the Demons like Tripurasuras (Three), Tarakasura, Namuchi, Vrutrasura are mentioned. Many interesting stories about their fights for superiority, wealth, power etc. are also given. We come across quarrels between Vak (Word) and Manas (Mind), Demons and Sun; co-wives Kadruva and Suparni, serpents and meters (Chandas) etc. There are interesting accounts of creation, sequence of the appearance of different creatures, animate and inanimate forms of existence, stories of spiders, dogs, fox, deer, liquor, thunder bolt, bamboo, musical instruments, cows, goats, stars, and their controlling deities, eclipses, seasons, habits of shaving, bathing, weaving etc., remarriage, sacrifices, food, special grass (Darbha), white-ants and many wide-ranging things–baffling, surprising, stimulating and ennobling. It is declared that the Vedas are infinite or unending (Ananta) and are compared to huge mountains (Yajurveda Brahmana, Prapataka). Vyasa had rearranged the available literature and classified it. He was credited with having written the Brahma Sutras and the 18 Puranas. Valmiki who wrote Ramayana, the first Epic, also appears as a character in the later part of the tale. So, we can surmise that the Rishis appearing in the several scriptures were also the authors to some extent. They considered themselves different from the Gods as also from men. They were the harbingers of prosperity and peace for Gods, men, animals etc. as can be seen from the final verse (mantra) of Purusha Sukta which is common to all the Vedas.

Long after the Vedic period, different schools of knowledge were founded by the sages who had insight into the philosophical purport of the Veda. Nyaya school was founded by Gowtama, Samkhya by Kapila, Yoga by Patanjali, Mimamsa by Jaimini, Viseshika by Kanada and Vedanta by Badarayana. The Advaita, Visishtadvaita and Dvita schools followed later. Along with the philosophical systems Tantra system has also been developed which involved different types of worship. Broadly, they fall into the three divisions of Saivism, Vishnavism and Saktism. Host of commentators and exponents emerged in all the systems of knowledge and Tantra. Voluminous literature had come into being. The kings patronized the developments and growth of the different schools of philosophy and systems of worship. All this was like the growth of a huge jungle. Some fail to see the wood for the trees and vice-versa. The powers of concealment (Avarana) and projection (Vikshepa) operate to confuse the seeker. Pure consciousness is possessed by Maya. In the cosmic or macro level it is known as Iswara and in the individual or micro level it is Jiva. The ultimate experience is described as Ananda or happiness, an inkling of which is obtained in deep sleep wherein there is no pain or suffering for the man. To remain in the state of bliss while being wakeful and exposed to the forces of creation, sustenance and destruction (Satva, Rajas, Tamas) is the aim of all the schools of knowledge. The methods to achieve this are differently given. Company of the wise (Satsanga) is given the highest place. As a corollary, the company of the ignorant and obstinate is the most painful thing. Pleasure is in the company of the wise. This underlines the all important value of 'respect for learning'. True learning, therefore, results in elimination of sorrow. To put it in a gross way, people should stop crying for and over things and happenings. We should inject cheerfulness into our life by conscious effort through all the available media. This will facilitate an attitudinal change which is vital for self-development. This is a major factor of value in the culture of the nation. Next in importance is the value of 'Dedication to duty'. Qualified and worthy people are keen to go away from the frustrating conditions in India where they cannot make a mark or prosper in their professions. We should ensure that a feeling to contribute to the improvement of things in the land of their birth is promoted by the elders who cannot disown the responsibility for the situation in the country. Our philosophy of sacrifice which Gandhiji fully exploited for winning freedom should be made to sprout again in the new-rich and power-hungry class of people which is a post-Independence phenomenon. Thus, pursuit of knowledge and excellence, respect for learning, cheerfulness and dedication to duty are the four vital ingredients for the growth of a society as conceived by the Rishis who laid the foundation for Hinduism.

The Preceptor or Guru is an important institution in Hinduism conceived as nuclei for the development of good human beings in the service of the society. The age of recluses is over. The Vedic Rishis themselves lived a normal life with families and children, as it was considered necessary to have a proper understanding of life. It may not be an exaggeration to say that others, like the present day bachelor swamis and babas, are unfit to give spiritual or moral instruction. The exceptions like Suka and Sankara can easily be explained as they were totally absorbed in the divine and were not having dealings with worldly people at all. Religious service got corrupted by unqualified people entering it without leading a regular life of the four Ashramas of Student, Householder, Anchorite, Renunciate (Vidyarthi, Grihasta, Vanasprasta, Sanyasa). I find that in the Veda, Upanishads and Puranas, the preceptors lived normal life of householders. The extreme case of boys becoming Sanyasis (like Sankara) is not to be accepted. Sankara who chose a wandering life, was a phenomenon by himself and should not be taken as an example. We have to restructure the system and revive the Vedic concept of a Guru. Much damage has been done in modern times by the bachelor swamis and babas who are not fit to impart religious instruction as per the Vedic system which is the true foundation of Hinduism. While Gita declares "Uddharet Atmanatmanam", Buddhism adopts it in toto in Dhammapada stating "By oneself one is purified". This overrides all other concepts including the final one of

Buddhism called Maggajina (Chunda Sutta). The true spiritual leaders who effectuated deliverance of the entire nation from ignorance and slavery into Effulgence and Freedom at the two historical points of time separated by more than a millennium are Sankara and Gandhiji. All others who appeared in between by different names and description cannot be given the same importance. Ramanuja, Madhwa and Vallabha are the three exponents who became Acharyas by dint of their originality. There are several beads through which runs the golden thread of Hinduism. We have to find a new meaning and purpose to this golden Heritage.

The Purusha Sukta which is recited in almost all the Hindu religious functions is found in all the four Vedas with slight variation. It deals with the origin and purpose of creation of the universe. It speaks of 21 categories in three stratas of seven each. Many interpretations have been given to suit the numbers. The earth, atmosphere and heaven (Bhuh, Bhuvah, Suvah) are the three stratas. The elements can be arranged in a periodical table of seven grades each on the basis of atomic weights. We can give different energies in the second strata, viz. (1) Radiation, (2) Light, (3) Electricity, (4) magnetism, (5) Heat, (6) Sound, and (7) Gravitation. Life can be treated in the third strata consisting of (1) Desire, (2) Will, (3) Memory, (4) Cognisance, (5) Decision, (6) Selection, and (7) Happiness (Ananda). Earth, Water, Fire, Air, Space, Time and Soul (Atman) are given fixed status with location (Dik) and mind (Manas) as variables. Several permutations and combinations are worked out relating man (Purusha) with Nature (Prakriti). Everything, Manifested and unmanifested, in this universe can be analysed in the light of three primary categories of (1) Particle (2) Energy and (3) Knowledge. The entire Vedic system is based on the spirit of cooperation which includes constructive competition as distinguished from ruinous conflict or wasteful dissipation. The Thinker is the pivot and all others are helpers in the different areas of execution. This is how society has been conceived. Proper education and skills are necessary for the professions taken up by the people. All philosophical speculations of the ultimate nature of things can be silenced or avoided if we fellow the true Vedic system of pursuit of excellence in the service of the world of man by promoting the right temperament and skills in the myriad facets of human activity for adding to the quality of life.

Hinduism gives utmost importance to young men and women in the building up of society. In ancient times, they learnt grammar (Panini), some Sutras, prose, verse and other subjects. "A healthy mind in a healthy body" was the norm. They get suitable appointments by going to the king's court and showing their talents. There are accounts that even girls were free to wear the sacred thread. It is very easy to understand the protection given to the section of the body containing the heart, lungs, lever etc. by the strong thread worn in position, apart from any religious significance. Probably, all students wore the sacred thread as it gives a feeling of dedication and protection to whosoever wears it as per the mantra. In Buddhism, the institution of nuns (Theri Bhikkunis) was developed, comprising of women with indomitable resolve, those seeking freedom from domestic trammels and grief-stricken persons. Young people are idealistic by nature and can be motivated for life. Given proper foundation they grow into worthy citizens, even as teeth are for life after the milk-teeth fall off. The Vedic literature and the epics stress the importance of cultivating the young people for the good of the society. Our society passed through many vicissitudes. Most rituals, religious exercises, symbols etc. have no relevance to-day. They are now serviced by toothless old people with self-interest. All the intellectual, dialectical and polemical theories and arguments have also been developed by many idle minds which should be discarded in toto without wasting further time on study and research into them. We should develop a vibrant work-philosophy as per the simple Vedic ideals. Many Vedic Mantras are obscure and cannot be discerned cogently. I have made a careful study of them. It no doubt helps to get by heart some minimum verses from the classics as they act like stimuli to unfold the genius of man. Gandhiji is a recent example of the result of this system of training. The flowers of Gandhism are being trampled by ill-informed and insincere people. The Chatak bird, it is said, flies up into the heavens after the egg falls down from the upper regions and gets hatched in the process, to regain its lost place high-up in the skies. This is the example given in Veda for young people to realise their proper place and make efforts for the upliftment of society. Hinduism is full of glorious examples for the youth of India. It is a perennial philosophy, nectar for life and goldmine of thoughts, all directed towards beneficial action leading to happiness and peace for the individual and the society everywhere.

Though Yoga was conceived in the context of acquiring super consciousness or union with the divine, it permeates the whole range of the personality including the external discipline. Curiously, physical discipline is given an important place in Hindu metaphysics. The Ashtanga Yoga has the first step of Asana or posture followed by other exercise leading to concentration and even intuition. Ergonomics is complementary to it wherein cleanliness (Soucham) is emphasised. This facilitates better communication, penetration and absorbtion of ideas. Mutuality, rapport, sympathy, empathy, cordiality etc. are facilitated. A kind of "human touch" is built into the situation. Students, teachers, workers, officers, speakers, listeners, doctors, patients, dignitaries, athletes, aspirants and all manner of people and activities come under its purview. I find that this aspect has not been properly appreciated in our society. To give an example from what is observed on TV, many of our top dignitaries are seen sitting with one leg dangling and the foot pointing towards the visitor, contrary to the level posture befitting the occasion. Though there is a superficiality of comradarie, the lack of basic discipline in the sitting posture betrays insensitivity. The Rishis laid great emphasis on such matters. The mind is a vast reservoir of impressions, experiences, impulses, sensations, processes etc. which reacts to every detail presented. It is like a special computer influencing the sub-conscious also. We can at least learn how to sit properly in all the varying situations in life, high or low, by educating our mind with the principles of Yoga! Following the basics in several externals has been prescribed by the sages. For example, the Tilakam (Bindi) worn in the centre of the forehead helps in proper attention to the person. For women, apart from the ornamental or decorative value in the Aesthetics of dress and appearance, it imparts dignity to the gaze of the perceiver. It serves as a subtle directional force. The tie worn in modern times as a central line from the neck to the navel also serves similar purpose. It is a beautiful concept. Examples can be multiplied. Suffice it to say that Yoga of Hinduism integrates the body culture and mind culture with the surroundings for the fulfillment of objectives. Ego problems are eliminated and the mind gets elevated. This is relevant and applicable to every situation and every person, high or low, throughout life. Only those who have risen spiritually to the highest state of liberation (Jeevanmukti) are not bound by these rules and they seldom bother to interact with worldly people or value their word. In my experience I have seen that such liberated souls also show concern for putting others at ease for creating an atmosphere of peace. Stories to the contrary about the turbulent or unruly behaviour of swamis, babas and saints (like those of the Naga cult at Khumba Mela) have to be discounted. The real Sadhu or Saint never loses temper or shows anger even for fun. This is the true spirit of Hinduism.

It is great to become a saint of knowledge in the true sense of the word and by Vedantic standards it means"knowing which all else is known". In my ambition, what I have chosen as the next best things is, to become a warrior of knowledge! This is a path of righteousness and courage and not one of meekness and crime. In Greek mythology, Prometheus stole the fire from Gods. Adam stealthily ate the apple. The basic difference in approach to the progress of morals between the West and the East in ancient times was in this standpoint. The doctine of "Survival of the fittest" was viewed from this angle in Hinduism. It is not a case of siding with the sinners or the weak. The attempt is to eliminate the need for pity, charity, weakness etc. It is like a war against ignorance, poverty, disease and other evils. It should not be misconceived as a war against the wealthy, healthy and prosperous people as in the Communist dogma whose chief priest, Karl Marx proclaimed "property is theft" which is sacrilegious when compared to Gandhiji's socialism contained in his statement "property is trust". Nietzsche, the great Western Philosopher, read the code of Hinduism by Manu and Placed it high above the Bible. He felt that Christ's Gospel died on the Cross with him and what followed was only the reverse of that "Gospel". It sounds so true when we find that war materials have filled the world and the human race is threatened with extinction under the patronage of Christianity. Fortunately it saved the world from Islamic swords (bombs). It is not difficult to refute the idea that war is a biological necessity. Hinduism has also been infected with some flaws of history (Islamic invasions, traitor kings, hypocritic leaders, escapist philosophers, false prophets, beggarly institutions), but at its roots it is based on universal love and human endeavour for prosperity and peace thorugh knowledge and understanding. To translate or realize these ideals what we need is not idleness, charity, vacant minds in meditation, blabbering babas, swindling swamis and such other anti-work elements but a vibrant work-force in every field of activity with faith in themselves and the eternal values of Hinduism as laid threadbare in this essay.

Life is a celebration and an instrumentality for still higher lives till an absolute state is attained. Life is not an evil to be despised or subjected to self-torture. It is not to be confused or mixed up with the plant and animal life of lesser nature. Nor is it to be viewed as an end in itself without any noble purpose other than materialistic enjoyment through the senses and sense objects. It is certainly not an animal existence with greed, fear, hatred, anger etc. inflicting harm on others and ultimately ending in death. Hinduism has evolved glorious principles for the happiness of man and good of the society. The Rishis devoted whole lives to unravel the mysteries of life and gave a positive, progressive and work-oriented philosophy which is known as Hinduism. In the modern context we can apply the ideas in the vital field of HRD also. By adopting an open and free system of management we can convert what is cynically thought as "forced labour" into an enjoyable experience of "free labour". The element of "willingness and cheerfulness" makes the difference. One of the greatest builders of modern India, late shri Mokshagundam Visweswarayya gave the correct slogan "industrialise or perish". If we do not inculcate the work values in all the employees from top to bottom it will result in the tragedy of "industrialise and perish". It will be like forcing people to commit thefts and then cutting off their hands as per the barbarous law of some countries in olden days! Luckily, the age of plunder and looting by hordes was over but the increase in population by leaps and bounds without economic growth is a continuing threat. Hinduism differentiates between crimes due to hunger (Apatdharma) and those committed by sense compulsions or uncontrolled senses. An accident is different from sabotage! We can prevent both by proper education and discipline. The entire complexion of industrial working can be changed by the new awareness of the values. Similarly, by adopting the Yogic theme of recreation we can make "Healthy people healthier". Both the above concepts are related in a way and we can organize peace programmes for the employees to instill the new awareness in them. By starting peace centres we can also serve the retired persons and general public by suitable extension programmes. I have drawn the inspiration from the principles of Hindu philosophy and Yoga and formulated the relevant scheme for the above purpose. 'peace farms' was the concept which I presented years ago of which 'Peace Centres' formed the core. Through them, the eternal, universal and ennobling values of Hinduism can be demonstrated and spread throughout the world.

GREETINGS

Wish you all the happiness and a host of hearty joys
Fulfilment of lofty aims and desires of your choice;
If healthy seeds are sown in time the plants will grow so fine
For lovely flowers to sprightly spring and delicious fruits to bring;
The sun-god sprinkles ripened rubies and the Moon silver yields;
The humble farmer happily harvests the rich golden fields;
The cowherd tends his countless cattle in shady verdant vales

'Milk and honey' literally flowing, the Country then regales;
The Koel sings its mirthful songs surely on the morrow
Let's light the brightening candles and banish all the sorrow;
Nights and Days will keep on rolling, life is also fleeting;
Let's make this a memorable year with kindness, goodwill and cheer;

– Muchimilli

2

Hinduism

Foundation of Hinduism

The four Vedas viz., Rig, Yajur, Sama and Adharvana, the most ancient scriptures in the world, were the foundation for Hinduism. Their authorship was unknown and attributed to divine revelation. They are propagated only by word of mouth throughout the millenniums ensuring accuracy in an ingenious method of recitation. The word Veda means "to know".

The Vedas are divided into 4 parts, viz. Samhitas, Brahmanas, Aranyakas and Upanishads.

The Rig Veda has 1028 Hymns divided into 10 Mandalas of varying length containing a total of 10,586 verses of which only about 150 deal with philosophy as such. The Yajur and Sama Vedas are mostly repetition of Rig Veda with accent on sacrificial rituals. The Adharvana Veda deals with magical spells, witchcraft, cures, warfare etc. The Rig Vedic Hymns are in praise of different deities. The Sukta 1-164 of Rig Veda gives the example of two birds sitting on a figtree (Pippala) with one eating the fruit and the other simply witnessing. This is the spiritual analysis of a human being with both the soul and God being together. Again, the Rig Veda contains the

Hymn propounding the truth to be one but explained as many by the learned (Ekam Sat). There are Vedangas, Upa Vedas and Darsanas which dealt with different aspects of the knowledge flowing from the Vedas. We have to sift the material available and pursue the clear spiritual stream of thought which alone leads to the ultimate goal of realization. We are missing the wood for the trees, the garden for the plants, the elephant for the legs, trunk etc. Moreover , the whole is more than the sum total of the parts! Many thinkers, saints, commentators and others who drew inspiration from the ancient texts have given varied versions of their understanding resulting in vast differences in practice over the centuries of human growth. Having studied almost all scriptural texts with original commentaries of the great Acharyas, the author finds that there is no need to further the hair-splitting exercise of individual commentaries through books and speeches on the several Upanishads or other spiritual texts. We have to integrate them and give a universal outlook to subserve the cause of peace.

Concepts and Philosophies of Hinduism

Originally, six major branches of science were recognized as extension of Vedas, like medicine, astronomy etc. Later on, 64 branches of knowledge and arts were developed. It was estimated that there are 84 lakhs of species. Man is the highest form of evolution.

The spiritual Law is expansiveness and not shrinking into fanatical dogmas. It is also a romantic concept of total absorption like the flow of rivers into the ocean. the garden has many flowers. The fabric has to have many threads. The monotony of a single book or form or even formlessness can be restrictive or even destructive. This explains the Hindu pantheon. The joy of fulfillment is varied and should meet the needs and capabilities of beings at different levels of evolution and development. Even tastes and moods are different. Otherwise, it tantamounts to death, stagnation or animal existence. There are many unique features of this land, the rivers, purity of the waters, the range of flora, fauna, climate etc., compared to others. Modern science has established the validity of the truths hitherto sustained by faith and custom. As we progress, more will be revealed in confirmation of them.

The Hindu tradition gave out glorious principles. Human effort is always insisted for human progress and not idle rituals sacrifices etc. as devised by the priest-class E.g. (1) Kritam mey dakshine haste–Adharvana Veda; (2) Krishito Nasti Durbhiksham–Mahabharat; (3) Karamaneyvadhi Karaste-Gita. It is good to remember that the Hindu Godesses of Wealth and Wisdom (Lakshmi and Saraswathi) represent the Hindu thought. The great law-giver Manu set the highest place for women in Hindu society. It's more than mere physical equality. Rama opted for Monogamy and gave a new direction to family life though the scriptures allowed polygamy. The author can go on expatiating on innumerable other issues and quote with authority from all the scriptures.

Generally speaking, in Hindu metaphysics, Epistemology (theory of knowledge) and Ontology (theory of existence) are not separately treated. We have the revealed and acquired aspects of knowledge. The sources are mainly threefold–(1) Pratyaksha (Apprehension). (2) Anumana (Inference) and (3) Sabda (Intuition). We need not go into the details of different schools of philosophy like-Mimamsa, Ganapatya, Nyaya, Samkhya, Viseshika, Yoga, Vedanta and the Agnostic offshoots like Buddhism, Jainism, Charwaka etc. The entire body of philosophy has been given the scriptural, logical and ethical base through the Prasthanathrayi of the Upanishads (Sruti), Brahmasutras (Nyaya) and the Gita (Smriti) on which the great Acharyas, Shankara, Ramanuja and Madhwa gave comprehensive commentaries. After a deep study of their works and the further commentaries following the methods of thesis, antithesis and synthesis, we can safely conclude that Active Peace is the ultimate goal. The various prescriptions (Vidhi) and prohibitions (Nishedha) found in Vedas and subsequent treatises aim at this objective of establishing peace within and without. In common colloquial parlance all the laborious exercises of the various philosophical schools amount to nothing more than stating the fact of the "Rice-grain being in the Paddy shell". Volumes of books on the minute aspects of separate texts of Upanishads and other philosophical treatises would show lack of real purpose beyond the pedantic exhibition of scholarship, smacking of redundancy, duplication, obsolescence and stagnation in all the spheres viz. hedonistic, legalistic and idealistic. Simplification, integration and unification has not been attempted in right earnest which was the sole cry of anguish of the Vedic seers. The author has attempted to humbly present in a capsule, a bird's-eye view of Hinduism with a modern SWOT analysis (Strengths, Weaknesses, Opportunities and Threats). The ABC of Hinduism is "Always Be Cheerful!" and "Able, Bold and Courteous."

The four-fold Veda which forms the basis for Hinduism deals both with the properties of Matter and the Charecteristics of Life with a symbolism and analysis of its own requiring different understanding and interpretation than a verbatim and parrot-like approach. There are, no doubt, few passages called 'Astra' which when chanted, directly invoke the Devas or natural forces animated by the note, frequency, quality, nature, volume etc. of the sound. They produce a state of mind. The sound-webs are to be seen in the light of Chandas and Siksha. Vyakarna and Nirukta deal with the science of language and the code. Panini and Yaska dealt with them respectively. The Jyotisham associated with Veda is different from the present materialistic Astrology. Taittiriya Siksha refers to Adhijyotisham. Likewise, Agni, Apah, Vidyut and Aditya have different meanings than ordinarily attributed to them, e.g. Agni is not merely the ordinary fire. You have the Jatharagani (Chemical), Naciketa (Mental), Vaiswaanara (Respiratory), etc. The crude symbolism of putting materials into the fire in the name of God is misleading. The Vedic system dealt with the various energy concentrations and their utility. Kalpa deals with the procedural part of Yagna. Asana, Mudra, Pranayama, etc. help in the process of self-evolution. Karirik Esti deals with the seeding of the clouds for rain. Rajasuyam is directed at the enemy and Vajapeyam aims at producing more food. Several such rituals have to be reinterpreted and recast to suit the present needs, the paramount principle being to create techniques to transform thought and life, using material and sound energies. In ancient times, people lived in awe and fear of the elements and forces of nature and tried to pacify them by all sorts of utterances and offerings. The overgrowth submerged the essentials. The forms dried up the substance. Rituals of all faiths need radical reform.

The Vedic system dealt with the mechanics of change with the harmonization of thought, action and experience to evolve into higher states of existence. Matter and life are related through the Five Elements – (1) Akasa or Space with sound or hearing , (2) Vayu- Air or movement with feeling or touch; (3) Tejah- Light or fire with sight (4) Apah–Water or fluid with taste and (5) Pridhvi–Matter or earth with smell. Intuition, desire, thinking ability, will and memory are the subjective faculties related to the above material elements respectively. Thus, creation and matter are intertwined with the unfoldment or evolution of life. The ultimate goal is set as total liberation (Urvarukamiva Bandhanat) and absolute enjoyment or bliss (Ananda or Amruta). The words Ahuti, Agni and Deva (oblation, fire and God) have to be understood in a proper perspective. Different Mantras are associated with different Agnis. Aswamedha is not horse sacrifice. Aswa means to grow to perfection: Medha means intelligence. Pasuh is not an animal but anything that can be seen or felt. Pandit Hari Shankar Joshi had done yeoman service in analyzing the true Vedic thought in his book 'Vedic Yoga Sastra'. The Rig Veda analyses the sound in different stages of Para, Pasyanti, Madyama and Vikhari. Thus, sound also comes under the definition of 'Pashu'. If we sublimate the entire Vedic systems and thought, we arrive at the conclusion that sacrifice is the foundation on which we have to build the human society. This is true socialism as different from the western individualism. The latter is now absorbing the Hindu ideal.

The several forms and names attributed to Almighty through the ages are different means to comprehend and experience the glory of the Supreme in its myriad facets. Hinduism sustains all and is like the backbone. It accepts and respects saintliness and enlightenment wherever and in whomsoever it is found. It includes all the excludes none. Every year, millions are born into the world and millions perish into oblivion. The noble purpose of human birth should not be lost in pettiness and selfishness. The true man accepts his position and works incessantly with faith in himself, adding to the quality of life in and around. This is the sure way for the peace and prosperity of mankind.

Neem tree was associated with Nimal (Chitanya-Sai Baba; Mango with Narayanatheertha–Potana: peepal with Buddha, Ramakrishna and others. Banyan is another important tree with saintly association. Tulasi is given the highest place in household plants. Growing such trees and plants was considered an important spiritual activity. It should be revived in the present times to promote the spiritual air. A study of Charaka Samhita and Sarangadhara Samhita would reveal the spiritual basis of Ayurveda. Apart from floral, fruit, food, medicinal, protective and decorative value of plants, trees and herbs, there is a spiritual purport or association. Hinduism gives extraordinary importance to Nature and Environment in a wonderful variety of ways including biotechnology and Genetic-engineering.

Who is a Hindu?

Experiments have revealed that the mind can be brought to rest by simple contemplation and meditation. Worship is an exhilarating adoration of the superhuman and benign images or representations and not of a mortal or a mundane symbol. The 15,000 million nerve cells in the human brain, 130 million of them in the eye and similarly in the ear react, absorb, align and delineate according to natural and creative patterns, tending towards tranquillity, happiness and peace. The sages discerned them by intuition and psychic experimentation and gave expression to them for the benefit of humanity. The forms of Gods and Goddesses were the result of their esoteric and mystical perception. The symbolism involved in certain forms drawn from nature like the monkey, elephant, lion, lotus etc. and reflected in the popular Gods of Hanuman, Ganesh and others has a mystical force on the human mind. Some strange familiarity, attraction and veneration towards the supreme is experienced in the process. A subtle communication or rapport is established with the creative elements of nature. The numerous and colourful Hindu festivals have also such human and natural significance besides serving the social purpose of unity in diversity.

Unfortunately, nobody has so far attempted to give a definition for the word "Hindu". As per orthodox or true classical requirement, every word must be given an etymological definition. That is the greatness of the Sanskrit language. It was the good fortune of the author that after extensive study and deep contemplation leading to intuitive understanding, he could arrive at the definition of the word "Hindu" as "Hinam Dushayati Va Durayati iti Hindu", i.e. a person who discourages evil and helps in its atonement. This definition answers the most stringent, orthodox and classical requirements of the Sanskrit language and our philosophical heritage. If accepted and followed by all, this will save us from the embarrassment and awkwardness of not being able to define who is a Hindu. Its catholicity will be welcomed by all.

The persistent prayer of a Hindu is for the prosperity of the human race. Even before 2500 B.C., Vedic utterance gave out the benediction:

> Let there be health and happiness in the world;
> Let there be auspiciousness everywhere;
> Let no one be afflicted with grief;

The above spirit permeates every throbing of the heart and every expression of thought of the seers and the successors to this date. As the above idea is borne out by all the scriptures and other literature of different religions all over the world, we can establish a common ground for universal peace and progress.

Why make distinctions before the supreme! Only certain physical or hygienic requirements may be reasonable. A TEMPLE OF God must be universal. We must build "universal temples" where all are accepted as belonging to one human family, thus proving love as the basis of religion and not hatred or ill will. Many meaningless external attributes have also acquired religious significance. It is time we discarded the cumbersome and unhygienic physical attributes and requirements which are hindering the spiritual life of people all over the world.

Veneration of the Cow- The Symbol of Prosperity and Peace

On analogy of an individual, a nation has an ethical subconscious mind which should not be destroyed or weakened. The foundation of Rama Rajya was traced to the protection of the cow, in Kalidasa's Raghuvamsa. We can certainly take some measures for proper feeding and protection of cows. The total gain to the nation physically, spiritually and sentimentally will far outweigh the supposed materialistic gain in treating them as mere food animals. It is good to remember the good old English saying "That country could be happy whose honest men could speak as loud as the scoundrels". Enough food can be produced from the numerous animal species; all animals can be multiplied and fully utilized; but, the cow can be spared. The disposal of dead and diseased cows can be refined and improved. Killing cows for food is like burning our clothes for warmth.

It may also be established that certain manias and incurable disease of psychic and genetic nature result form eating the cow. Some believed that lucoderma and leprosy were also such diseases. The human system has been so thoroughly tested according to Ayurveda over several centuries. This is a peculiar science by which we can establish the effects of different food materials on the human system. Physicians who deeply studied Ayurveda and treated many desperate cases confirmed the validity of the above statement. This may be one instance of truth being stranger than fiction to ordinary minds. We should have something as a National Pride also as a crest jewel of unbroken traditional values nurtured and cherished by the native genius of the people. Even a simple and toiling villager will laugh at the utter lack of sentiment and pity the irreligious and new-fangled attitude as matricidal. We will be humiliated if we try to dispose of our old mother who may become useless to us any longer; it is a repulsive thought.

One also gets an experience of being blessed while feeding a cow and serving it with veneration. Saints who tended cows testified the wonderful experience of this blessing. This is the secret of the enormous powers and charms of Lord Krishna. The scriptures have also warned of the curse and calamities to the land where cows are killed. A mystical truth was proclaimed by the sages which ca be experienced even now by any sincere person. A cow is imbued with divinity or the milk of divine kindness which is incomparable and unique. Deep insight into science, medicine, mysticism and the secrets of creation will prove that the cow should continue to be treated as Gomata and not as a mere animal. Like the sacred Tulasi plant, the cow, it can be established, emits radiation which purifies the spirit. Some physical ailments are mysteriously cured by rendering service to and living in the presence of a cow, taking its milk and bathing with its urine and dung. Even an invalid cow has immense gobar gas and fertilizer value compared to the negligible cost of its feed. Let us not spill the poison even if it is found in some quarters and ruin the physical, mental and spiritual health of the nation.

A simple study reveals the cow as an epitome of selflessness, meekness and purity in the entire creation and no animal or human being can be equated with it except one's own dear mother. The only sutra or injunction is "Gavo matarah, amaranatam sevitavyah" the meaning being, the cow is like the mother and should be served unto death. May the sensibilities of our children and the spiritual nerve of the nation be not destroyed. May the lord protect the backbone of our heritage. May we not be visited by the curse and calamities. May peace be unto all!

The Theme of Bhagavas Gita

If Rama was an embodiment of virtue supremely dedicated to Dharma in every action he performed, Krishna was a teacher par excellence imparting supreme wisdom in many words he uttered. Both were so enchanting and charming to look upon, contemplate and meditate. Their captivating beauty is varied and limitless. With even a little sincerity and imagination one can develop the awareness of their divinity followed by the thirst to drink the joy of transcendence. This culminates in Yoga without one being conscious of it. This helps us to discharge our allotted duties with added enthusiasm, dedication and competence. This promotes selflessness, peace and friendliness and curbs individual craving and purposeless living. This establishes that mankind is one and the only law is love of humanity. Harbouring even the slightest hatred towards fellowmen is bestiality; shedding evil intentions totally is true Wisdom; working ceaselessly for human well-being is divinity. This is the lesson of Gita. Can there be another teacher more loving and more glorious than lord Krishna! Like Rama, he proved his valour as the Supreme Lord by ruthlessly vanquishing all evil forces howsoever formidable they might be and brought peace and happiness to the faithful and righteous people. This was the test of Godhood. As proclaimed, he reappeared from time to time in different lands in different forms as the situation demanded but the lesson was only one, viz. love of humanity. This oneness in manyness can be symbolized as OM. It is our turn now to be so blessed and live up to our heritage.

The Concept of Rama Rajya

Of the millions of sounds and utterances, 'Ram Ram' proved too be the most powerful, mellifluous, musical, expressive, sweet, soothing, stable and sublime. It is miraculous that mere chanting of the word can give one the experience of spiritual inspiration as acknowledged by even atheists and agnostics. The science of Yoga brings about unity and harmony within and without. This oneness and manyness is symbolized in "OM" . Hinduism provides true strength when you are up against the wall of brutality or at the cross-roads of sin or in the fire of selfishness. It is common sense that a simple human being with weakness and without strength cannot save himself against formidable enemies. How can such a person save others? It, therefore, stands to reason that the supreme has to reveal himself in different lands and times as the need arose.

The process goes on and the cycle repeats itself. The only lesson is love of humanity.

Rama is the ideal before mankind. He was the first true integrator of the Indian subcontinent and giver of new values to individual and social life. As an epitome of sacrifice, he put down evil and upheld merit. Experience strengthens the testimony for truth.

Volumes have been written on the glory of Rama and Ramayana. Thousands of poets have been inspired by the great ideals set before them by the original and first poet Valmiki centuries before Christ.

The word 'RAMA' contains within itself the supreme power and its changing itself will impart wisdom and peace of mind, which has been confirmed by great Saints and Sages who never uttered untruth. It is up to us to accept their testimony and realize the fruits of their guidance. Just say 'Ram Ram Ram' and feel the miraculous joy sprouting in you. No esoteric initiation is necessary. One can utter the sacred name in any of the innumerable cherished forms. If a Super Computer is fed with the millions of words and utterance, 'Ram Ram Ram' will again prove to be the most powerful, mellifluous, musical, expressive, sweet, soothing, stable and sublime. It is now proved that the chanting of the Mantra "Ram Ram" produces some mysterious vibrations in the subtle body which will permeate the life-force and change the metabolism curing even heart disease miraculously. Several agnostics acknowledged the phenomenon after experimentation.

The great virtues of which Rama was an embodiment are beacon lights for the guidance of mankind eternally. The charm and enthralling situations of the great epic make us spellbound even today. The scenes depict tender and sublime emotions and varied aspects of individual and community life and ideals. May the sacrifices, virtues and dutifulness of Rama and Sita inspire us and our children towards leading a purposeful and happy life in the realization of Dharma, Artha, Karma and Moksha, i.e. Human action, well-being, excellence and fulfilment. These noble values will bear fruit if they are inculcated in childhood itself. Children born in this land are heirs to this glorious Universal Wisdom. May the Lord bless the faithful reader!

Our intelligence creates the differences. We, therefore, need wisdom which integrates and ennobles. Originality, creativity, meditation, super conciousness and intuition are some of its attributes. All the scriptures and pronouncements of the saints of yore convey the clear message of unity in diversity and urge upon us to realize and work for peace within and without. This concept was the foundation of Ramarajya which is acclaimed even to this day. As put by the great poet Kalidasa in Raghu Vamsam the king was taught the spiritual principle of Brahman or eternity i.e. what is lasting and what is changing– "Naya-Vidbhirnaverajni Sadasat Chopadarsitam". This is the secret for the hold Ramayana and Rama have on people to this day. Millions of poets and Thinkers have been inspired and captivated by this sublime idea which lay at the root of Ramayan, the first Epic in the world.

Individual freedom should not be allowed to be sacrificed by communal compulsion and fanaticism in matters of physical appearance, dress, postures, language, lockets, caps, headgear, bodywear etc. In terms of Article 25 of the Indian Constitution "Public order, morality and health" override all narrow attitudes and harmful habits in the practice of religion. Some carry symbols on their bodies which remind us of the heinous crimes committed in bygone days and they drink, dine and dance in merriment wearing them. Some pseudo-intellectuals sporting beards and living despicable lives contrary to all religious injunctions, have become self-appointed champions of religion. This land once belonged Lord Rama and no religious leader worth the name or his parents disowned this heritage. Gandhiji lived and died for "Rama Rajya", a glorious concept for the happiness and prosperity of the Indian masses.

Vedas, Upanishads, Puranas, Itihasas and Sutras-

The Basis of Indian Philosophy

From Ancient times, the sages probed into the why and wherefore of creation and brought out enlightened treatises in various forms as Vedas, Upanishads, Puranas, Itihasas and Sutras i.e., scriptures, aphorisms, epics, biographies and codes.

Universal and most sublime values for the peace and prosperity of mankind can be deduced from them. Bhagavad Gita is one such compendium par excellence, the quintessence given in the shortest and simplest scriptural texts in the world. The wisdom spread to other parts of the world. Even the language and words made an impact: Manava has become man; Hrudayam, heart, Hastam, Hand; Sarpa, Serpent; cow, cow; taru, tree etc. According to great Historians, ancient and modern, the Greeks came to the banks of Ganges to lisp a little knowledge. Emerson, Whitman, Rolland, Wilson, Bloomfield, Macdonnel, Frazer, Suzuki, Toynbee, Einstein, Brown, Caldwell, Campbell, Henry, Morris, Garbe, Huxley, Schopenhauer and Haldane paid glorious tributes to the spiritual genius, profound philosophy, literary grandeur and cultural ethos of Hinduism. One marvels at the undisputed testimony given by Yuan Chwang, Fa Hsien, Macro Polo, Winternitz, Macdonnel, Elphinstone, Strabo, Tod, Rufus Jones, Royle, Garrison, Maculay, Gilbert, Malcolm, Megasthenes, sir Thomas Munro, Al Beruni, Fazal, Conti, Pierre Loti, Murray, Vincent Smith, Williams, Woodroffe, Lin yu Tang, Nakamura, Neibuhr and many others.

The only goal which was pursued with supreme dedication by the Vedic Seers and which is set for each and every soul is to progress from ignorance to truth; darkness to light and from death to immortality. On this was based the gamut of Indian Philosophy. Gandhiji in modern times had also drawn inspiration from a similar idea in Western Philosophy as expressed in the lines "in the midst of untruth, truth persists; in the midst of darkness light persists and in the midst of death life persists."

A purposeful and diligent study of all the scriptures, lives of the saints and different scientific and spiritual theories about creation, leads us to the one and only conclusion that our little lives can be made sublime by our own exertions and will. We should consciously broaden our outlook towards life by remembering the impermanence of our possessions and sharing with others whatever advantage we have by virtue of our birth or position. Is it not a fact that all the kings, rich and strong who fought and lived seeking only the pleasures and comforts of life had all perished without exception? It is reported that Alexander the Great, as death-wish, kept his empty palms outside his coffin to prove that nothing avails and that he was leaving empty-handed. All the possessions and wealth that one can think of is mere tinsel unless it serves to mitigate selfishness and help in promoting cleanliness, health, goodwill and harmony in the world. "I don't keep anything, but give back Tenfold" is a mystic statement. "Many are called but few are chosen" is the Lord's assurance.

One wonders at the remarkable conceptualization, blending and reconciliation of "Science and Values" as also of time and the World achieved by the Sages which is eluding the modern scientists and which is the latest pursuit and the ultimate goal of the present day Nobel Laureates. For Example, in Adharvana Veda, it was declared that 'time creates the world or space' ("Kalo Srujati Bhutalam",). This is the pinnacle of modern scientific postulation. Every achievement of the western world today can be traced to some vital contribution in our ancient wisdom; e.g. the number zero in Maths, Surgery in Medicine, Polestar in Astronomy, catalyst in Chemistry Atom in Physics, Extra-Sensory Perception in Psychology, Democracy in political Science, Essentialism in Socio-Economic Theory, etc. Foundations, physical and mental, were laid as it were, for the growth of a great and noble civilization on earth and not a mean and destructive one. But at some point, lost in antiquity , there was a break, a flood, sabotage or distruption. Slavery followed. The gems, seeds, and the elixir have to be salvaged from the debris and the weeds. Unfortunately, the predictive astrology has exploited the gullibility and eagerness of people. The predictions of idlers, unlike the unfailing blessings of saint astrologers of yore, have become rampant, making the people inactive, apprehensive, pessimistic, negative and fatalistic. This militates against the Karma theory and betrays lack of faith in oneself or in the Supreme. Despite our acclaimed and ancient heritage, subjugation, proselytisation and alien indoctrination have caused considerable degeneration.

Hinduism and Other Religious

Religion is not slavery to dead habits. Festivals may continue to be celebrated in so far as they provide for the creativity, entertainment, exhibition, participation and celebration of events in the life of the society. They lend charm and all sections rejoice in them. Given the opportunity and relevant education a human being will try to know the truth and live peacefully. This will mitigate the fanatical farce and spiritual pollution. Forced habits are incompatible with the joy in the pursuit of divinity. How to sit, stand or saluté in prayer is not so important as the purpose of invocation. Artificial barriers and narrow personal cults do not represent true religious activity. Freedom and tolerance are the hallmarks of a noble religion. Improvement of the quality of life is its motto; work is worship, its formula; liberation is its goal.

The aim and purpose of all religions is to make man happy and prosperous. The progress of Science & Technology is also related to better living conditions and enjoyment in life. In the beginning, when society was in a primitive stage, man had to struggle against Nature to provide for himself and his survival. Gradually, common interests emerged. Greater strength was found in togetherness. The peculiar features of environment an climate moulded the aspirations. The external features of life, such as dress, eating habits, greeting, gathering, disposal of dead bodies etc, were all pragmatically devised and developed to suit local conditions. Some tried to probe into the why and wherefore of creation. The variety, many-sided splendour, the regularity of events like sunrise, phases of the moon, seasons etc; cyclical forces in evidence likes snow, rivers, ocean, clouds, rain etc. provided inspiration. As there are degrees and differences in the quality of endowments in nature, so also some thinkers commanded greater grasp and gave theories of their understanding.

People, whose ancestors were devotees of Lord Rama throughout the length and breadth of India as an integrated nation have forgotten their moorings. It is stated that the founders of Sikhism like Guru Nanak and Guru Gobind Singh accepted Rama and claimed descent from him. The Guru Granth invokes the names of Rama, Hari and other Gods and

Godesses in thousands of places. Nanak prescribed only the three-fold path of 1) sat kah 2) Vand Chak and 3) Ram Jap. Guru Gobind worshipfully wrote the books "Ramavatar" and "krishnavatar" as also in praise of mother Durga. Likewise, Buddhism and Jainism have been considered to be off-shoots of Hinduism. Unfortunately, the fanatics as also the Psuedo-Secular people in India are indifferent to its noble heritage. Fortunately, Hinduism has the resilience in the native roots.

THE PATH

It's never late to make amends
And repent for your follies;
God is all kindness
And forgives his sincere devotees.
That man is great who clings to His feet
In despair or devotion so complete
For, if the lord is pleased and notes his fate
Emperors and angels scramble to his gate.
Reap the lasting happiness of heaven
Million-fold than all your mundane possessions make;
Have courage to cut asunder
The bonds of habit and blunder,
Unlock your conscience when all darkness will part
With the key of devotion cast out of your heart;
That will the highest wisdom to you impart
And unfold the Real, clear as a chart.
Your life is measured by the breaths you hold
In fealty for His grace with fervour untold;
Your wealth is measured by the tears that rolled
When you cried for the Lord with anguish untold.
Turn Your-self unto Him when awake or asleep
By so training your thought His company to keep;
Discard the superficial and delve into the deep
When the radiant pearls of devotion you shall reap.

– Muchimilli

3

Spiritual Values and Yogic Excellence

Spiritual Values

Human beings have to engage themselves in meritorious actions to deserve the real peace and happiness which are endowed on a superior soul. In such a state, material considerations lose significance. It is, therefore laid down that greed destroys progress and peace. Unfortunately, several people are engaged in accumulating assets for generations of their descendants making them snobs and denying them the opportunity to evolve on their own merit. There are no, no doubt, exceptions which can be attributed only to the aiscrimination and wisdom derived through meritorious deeds. The miserable conditions in India despite the vast rich natural endowments are the result of this wrong direction in the employment of wealth by selfish, ignorant or condemned souls. The remedy lies in revolutionising the concept of patronage and seeking meritorious souls for running the affairs of the State. A systematic dissemination of spiritual values can improve the general standards of judgement in locating such souls of talent and concern for public good ignoring selfish gains.

With a little effort everyone of us can realize the supreme importance of our own life in the fact that there is what can be called 'innate wisdom' or sensibility in each of us. This is variously termed as soul, conscience, spark of divinity etc. Our effort should be to preserve this "inner light" which alone gives the dignity and value to our life. The totality of this human element constitutes the ultimate reality. Therefore, it is necessary that instead of working at cross purposes, all our knowledge, sciences, exertions, institutions, systems and thoughts should concentrate on this sole principle which is the summum bonum of life. Then, we can never think of harming our fellow human beings by word or deed. We shall respect their feelings and sentiments; share our thoughts with them. We shall worship at religious places without rancour or ill will. We will not ban others from visiting our temples, mosques or churches if we regard them as divine. Our destiny is one and the same. We shall ennoble our lives by establishing this unity of thought and action in our lives.

Human being is the highest from of evolution amongst species. Even amongst humans, there are different stages. People are born into different circumstances with different faculties or inherent abilities. This cannot be easily explained except as being a result of past actions linked with genetic placement in the total scheme of living beings. Life is considered to be an independent force interacting with the material principle of creation. The soul is conceived as part of the primeval creative energy which split itself by its own will into beings. Thus, every soul partakes of the universal whole but is clouded in the peculiar material existence. A deep and thorough understanding of this genesis shows that the 'soul' of creation is limited to the human beings whereas the lesser forms of life like animals, insects, plants etc. have only physical life as contrasted with spiritual life.

Much thinking has been done as to how to reconcile the two apparently conflicting roles of activity-material and spiritual. The minimum that has to be ensured to make the birth as a human being worthwhile can be given in two words, "Be good: do good". Everyone can easily experience within oneself what is called conscience. Its voice is clear and distinct. It is always heard and 'goodness is in proportion to our harkening to it. The value system' of society should also be based on proper discrimination to avoid evil. Here lies the distinction between crime and sin. It is the privilege and prerogative of mankind to harness nature and its resources for the betterment of life. This depends on how we utilise our time. Should there be place in our hearts for hatred at all when we see that all persons are to die ultimately whatever be their language, colour, creed etc. The little 'ego' is playing havoc with all individuals. One should totally rid himself of the contamination and negative thinking. When the supreme gets assimilated, the religious compulsions, outward appearances, forced habits and fanatical practices will simply disappear. Once this awakening dawns on the human mind, just as the sunrays dispel the different shades of darkness and the fears attendant therein, we will begin to look upon every human being as a fellow traveller with friendliness and without illwill. This alone is true scientific temperament.

There are many who believe that there is no place for spiritual thought in administrative, governmental or management systems. This is the modern idea of professionalism. It is like saying that the active hands and mouth are more important than the silent backbone and the breath. "Give unto Caesar what is his and to God what is God's". The dichotomy of the State and the Church was keen. The upper hand of state power gave rise to doctrines like 'the king can do no wrong'. The brute power of the rulers can probably be brought under the Biblical saying: The lamp of knowledge cannot be lighted where the winds of foolishness blow too strong". To the Western World the idea of Philosopher-Kings was an ideal. In India, however, alongside the concept of the king being the fountain-head of justice, there was a system of spiritual tutelage for the rulers who never dared to disobey the sages and their counsel. Far from that. Lord Rama was himself characterized as the embodiment of righteousness "Ramo Vigrahavan Dharmah" but his humility was exemplary. King Solomon was another example in mythology for such wisdom.

A sincere commitment by every individual to evolve spiritually into a good human being is the fundamental pre-requisite for the progress of a nation. The sprit of living for others and helping the 'good' selflessly is the backbone of our culture whereas the present trend is a reversal of it when we find that utter selfishness and torturing of the truly meritorious have become rampant. A pseudo-culture of false humility, sycophancy, deceit, commercialisation and exploitation of artistic talents and women., idle pursuits and speculation, parasitical occupations in astrology, politics, religion etc. is cutting at the roots of a dynamic, progressive and action-oriented society which has been envisaged by our forbears as also the Founding Fathers of our Constitution. Mere lip-service to the ideals set before us has become a phenomenon in all walks of life, domestic and public alike. This has to be changed.

Mankind is now in the final state of evolution. As such, subjectivity and faith have come to be accepted by the best of minds. Bertrand Russel, probably the most well-read person of his century, has confessed in his book "My Philosophical Development" that he had literally thrown away all his books on Mathematics and took to pascifism. Einstein, the greatest scientist of the century, adopted a spiritual attitude after his experiments on the Unified Field (Life and Times.). His remark that future generations would not believe that a person like Gandhiji walked on this earth in flesh and blood is a spiritual evaluation of man. Immanuel Kant showed the evolution of his mind in "Critique of practical Reason" accepting the Supreme or Absolute will. The theory of Transmigration and immortality of soul found support from early thinkers of the present day geniuses irrespective of their place of birth, colour, creed, etc. Death is thus an opportunity to evolve, being an event in eternal life. According to Kant, the general experience being that the virtuous suffer and the wicked thrive, the balance is struck in afterlife. Is this inexorable? It is mystical that evil-minded people have an upper hand in reaching for power. This is also the Karma theory necessitating God to come down as an Avatar at the end. How far Euthanasia can reverse or rearrange the law, it is difficult to say! It is escapism to leave it to an Avtar or Mahatma without doing our duty. We will do well to accept that mankind is one large family with vibrant souls seeking peace as the ultimate goal. To contribute to this common cause one should consciously exert to increase the peace-content in his or her own life.

Our ancient Rishis, Gurus or Saints never expected us to appear and behave like primitive people in the changed circumstances of peace and freedom. They always valued and advocated the qualities of the mind and heart which are the essence of true religion. Everyone cannot be godly but one can be clean. It is, therefore, said that "cleanliness is next to godliness".

Universal Love – The Message of All Spiritual Leaders

Jesus was an embodiment of love. Consider his words, particularly those which he uttered when being crucified with torture "Lord, forgive them, they know not what they do". This is still being done by the war-mongers of today! Mohammed had nothing but compassion for the poor and was against their exploitation. Some of the Suras of Koran bear this out. Zarathustra, Buddha, Mahavira, Tao, Nanak and the host of other great religious leaders had divine qualities and supreme love for mankind. We need not become fanatical in following their words, leaving out the wisdom contained in them. After deeply studying their lives and works one feels that, had they lived to-day they would have felt shocked and wept to see the fanatical farce, pollution and primitive practices indulged in (ostrich-like) by people all over the world inspite of modern knowledge and scientific progress. The tender sentiments and noble emotions in all religions are different from the hard and harmful injunctions or prescriptions of the self-centered and ignorant priest class. We have to take guidance from enlightened souls who have dedicated their lives for the service of people through penance and self-denial. They have farsightedness and universal love untainted by the pettiness of intellectual wranglings and rigidity of rituals. We have to fulfill their hopes. Einstein postulated that the highest goal for creative people is to promote what he called the

"Cosmic Religious Feeling" which is free from dogma. He was profoundly influenced by the Advaitic or Non-dualistic Philosophy.

Success is expected to bring modesty. Newton stated "if I have seen further, it is by standing on the shoulders of giants". Dr. Radhakrishnan admitted his own limitations, philosophical and linguistic. Jesus told his disciples "Unless you change and become like children you will never enter the kingdom of Heaven". Mian Tansen, when asked about his life's achievement, said that he could grasp a little of one musical note "Gandhar Swar Ki Kuchh Pehchanhi Hi". Such is the ocean of creative genius. Our saints have assimilated the vast ocean of knowledge and gave us the benefit of their insight.

Love is the basis and meaning for life. A heart with love finds fulfilment. All religions worth the name are founded on love. The great thinker, Bertrand Russel took the view in his book "Why I am not a Christian" that the basis of religion is fear in its various aspects. Karl Marx postulated that religion is the opium of people and an escapist's excuse. Several great thinkers and reformists have gone on record with such critical observations against religion. Unfortunately, the course of religion in different parts of the world fell into the hands of narrow-minded priests, Mullas, Swamys and other religious leaders, who distorted the norms of the founders. Christ, Mohammad, Buddha, Mahaveera, Zarathustra, Tao, the ancient Vedic seers, Sankara, Nanak and all the founders of religion and religious institutions had nothing but love for humanity as can be seen from the scriptures and their sayings. Even an iota of the love they had for all people will transform the present day creeds, sects, denominations etc. which are dividing the human family.

The intellectual powers of the modern man are greatly enhanced by the exposure he has for advanced knowledge. But the will to overcome selfishness and develop universal love is poor. A quotation from Gandhiji shows his deep concern for the workers. "If I am appointed dictator for one hour... I would... compel owners to produce human conditions for their workmen and open refreshment and recreation rooms where they would get innocent drink and innocent entertainment". There is also his famous quotation "A customer is the most important visitor on our premises... we are dependent on him. He is doing us a favour by giving us an opportunity to serve him." This wisdom is essential for the revival of our nation. The vested interests against such freedom and consideration have been condemned even from the beginning of commercial society. Adam Smith in the Wealth of Nations referred "to the danger arising from the insolent outrage of furious and disappointed monopolists" in dealing with free world trade. Conservative like Paul Samuelson and Friedrich Von Hayek (Nobel laureate) have advocated free trade for economic growth. Thus at national and international levels in different areas touching the economic life and growth of people, a new management culture has to be evolved individually and collectively.

The people of the world are but one family (Vasudhaiva Kutumbakam); may all the people of the world enjoy peace and prosperity (sukhino bhavantu). Many such glorious passages ring in our ears as we read through the ancient texts. After extensive study and research, the author has compiled the names of more than 200 sages and saints of different faiths, religions and denominations who are the brightest stars in the Indian firmament. The only lesson to be learnt from them all is, Love of Humanity.

Yoga and Yogic Excellence

A deep study of the lives of leaders of religious movements and saints in the service of mankind would confirm that there is an under-current of commonness in their thoughts and humaneness in their approach beyond the physical limitation of their being. It is usually attributed to seemingly external inspiration mostly of divine origin. The uncertain or inexplicable nature of their experiences, actions and utterances was broadly termed as mysticism. But, interestingly, it would appear that even in the case of great thinkers, rationalist philosophers, poets and even politicians and administrators, whether it is acknowledged or not, their greatness can be attributed to the Yogic excellence which they have acquired in the process of their pursuits. The great Rishi, Patanjali, gave expression to this phenomenon and rationalized it as a psychic result. He named it as "Pratibha" in his treatise "Yoga Sutra" and defined it as a self-propelling force which leads a person forward after the initial education or discipline. Gita also lends support to the above observation in several places, the most striking pronouncement being "Yogah Karmasu Koushalam". A true Yogi applies himself to his assigned wordly duties with meticulous care and does not indulge in idleness or preaching passivity or inaction. This distinguishes him from the parasites in human form who thrive on others. We need a new yogic work force called "Peace Persons".

When Jesus declared that he and His Father were One it was an instance of attainment of union which is basic to yoga, as the etymological meaning of the word itself reads "Yujir Yojane" i.e, "To unite is Yoga". Similarly, Guru Nanak merged into the supreme and realised the Yogic union when he uttered the number 13 while counting the weighment of goods in the shop for, the word "Tera (13) in Hindi means also "Yours" and he instantly transformed himself as belonging to the Lord. Uttering the word Tera meant for him "I am yours, my Lord". This intensity, purity and identity cannot be an ordinary experience. Here again, we find the explanation in yogic thought which states "yogaha chittavritti nirodhah". It follows that the supreme is reflected in the pure mind which is devoid of vibrations and vagaries. It may appear to be begging the question if it is thought that yoga precedes the realization or is the cause for the effect. Curiously, it is the cause and effect in one or an end in itself. Yoga consciousness is exclusive which means that nothing else exists. In that way it can even be said to be all-inclusive. This is like the 'unified field' theory of Einstein which is all-encompassing.

Then, one may ask, what is the secret of the power of Yoga if it is all-pervasive. A simple answer can be found in the phenomenon of light which is plain and soft whereas its derivative 'Laser' is unique and immensely powerful. A Yogi has this laser technique ingrained in his actions and words, nay, in his very being. Prophet Mohammed had acted with such power when he ordered the demolition of the palatial building of a citizen because it was contrasting with the poverty all around. His compassion for the poor and tenderness of his heart are to be properly understood to appreciate the spirit of his words. Is not a diamond different from charcoal though both are of carbon content!

The Buddha, Mahavira, Zoraster, Sankara, Ramanuja, Madhwa, Bahaullah, Confucius, Gandhi and a host of great souls who are beacon lights of wisdom to this day, had all experienced the Yogic power in them which urged them forward in the path of Truth and service to mankind. They are all one in essence. But the followers have rigidified the norms and attached undue importance to slogans and symbols. Thus we have built walls, boundaries and barriers amongst the earthlings called humans. Yoga can unite us again as a universal human family. It does not require great intelligence to imagine the horrors of human misery which will be let lose in a nuclear warfare. The present stock of arms and ammunition all over the world speaks of the degeneration of our intelligence and understanding. In the medieval world, the conquests were the order of the day as part of the struggle for survival. Their ambitions were short-sighted and limited to their own glorification at the expense of others' lives. National Barriers have no meaning now and fighting for racial supremacy etc. is clearly barbarous and the trend has to be reversed so that all humans are accepted as members of one global family.

It would also be interesting to record the different experiences of a yogi as he progresses. Some are very subtle requiring keen observation but some can easily be discerned. The sense faculties become sharpened at times to a point of suffering e.g. even small sounds get magnified and become unbearable; light becomes glaring, sight of suffering in any form brings tears and he partakes; he would be inclined to be aloof, avoiding notice or company; worldly talk or affairs would not interest him; he becomes childlike. On the contrary, on occasions he would become stoic, indifferent and supremely tolerant, taking things in his stride. His words and manners are informal; his presence itself is soothing and sanctifying. He may not show awareness of his powers of healing, cognition or other extrasensory perceptions (ESP). But generally, he would not brook any insult to his dignity, probably feeling the presence of the Supreme in him. However, anger is avoided as it is considered to be a sign of immaturity in a person.

The Yogic expression has its own special stamp because it is pure and sublime. Without effort it takes highly technical literary forms. The words mould themselves like gold in the hands of the divinely inspired yogis. A reading of the great works like Bible, Koran, Granth Sahib, Ramayan etc. convinces us that this is the simple truth. Even now, in modern times, we can come across exalted literary forms. See the simple lines expressing the supreme yogic thought by the modern poet Muchimilli.

"Before the blazing sun of Brahman
I lighted the candle of my life
And into the deep and deathless ocean
I delivered the drop of my life."

Yogic excellence can also be found in the scientific field and purely materialistic or social sciences also, because the authors, scientists or specialists have truly attained that state of dedication and union peculiar to Yoga.

Yoga which etymologically means "To unite (yujir yojane)" has the sole aim of leading man to this Supreme understanding. Deep and exhaustive study and discipline would also lead to a state of intuition and Extra sensory perceptions (ESP).

After a general analysis, it may be concluded metaphorically that to achieve progress, the strong oak tree of society should be allowed to put forth its best sprouts upwards towards the Heavens and achieve the true Yogic union with the Supreme. In practical terms, we should generate a National Consciousness through Education and Public Media that our leaders should be well-informed people of vision, sacrifice, dedication and devotion to the noble cause of building up modern India as envisaged in the Constitution. This is National yoga which will bring about the union of the people with the national objectives and this is the first step towards Universal Yoga or union of Mankind. To reconcile the traditional with the modern is indeed a difficult task. To bring to bear the scientific temperament on our thinking and way of life requires great effort.

Hindu thought and tradition produced exceptionally great men of morality, spirituality and love. Equally astounding was the intellectual eminence of many of them. They truly presented as Alpha and Omega of human knowledge which can be abbreviated as AOM. It covers the whole range from Euthenics to Solipsism, from death to immortality, from atom to universe. Though one may find certain Battology, Idolatry, Superstitions etc, as criticized by the 'Big-talkers" and "High-up philosophers" in the words of Vivekananda, we should not "throw away the baby with the water" as the saying goes. The attempt has been to develop the soul from within, which is the true meaning of education, (Latin Educo, to educe or develop from within). In other words, the stress is 'to make people good by choice' which was Tolstoy's idea of the highest-purpose of art. The rituals may be compared to the bark which is different from the tree. With the emergence of some Theomaniacs and cult-figures, faith has become perverted and lost credibility with the intelligentsia. We have to carefully analyse the purpose of religion and give it the real direction for the good of mankind as originally conceived by the Vedic seers to make the world a safe place for good people to live in and grow. In this context, it is worthwhile to reproduce below certain lines from an earlier work of the author, "PEACE AND PURPOSE IN HUMAN LIFE" in order to bring out the central theme of religion:

"Beethoven had rightly observed that it is only through untiring use of our faculties with which we can revere the Creator. No purpose would be served in repeating parrot-like, the same shibboleths and quotations from the so-called authorities. We must consciously make efforts to rise above the shackles of words into the world of reality and peace. Action is the key to success in many spheres as also for unlocking the mystery of life. All doctrines which advocate passivity and cessation of work are harmful. Fulfilment lies in the meticulous application to the duties and responsibilities in life irrespective of their range or reward. The person who has acquired the right understanding or liberation has to engage himself in beneficial work as enthusiastically as the ignorant or the material minded. Even a small step in the right direction shall be regarded as a big leap compared to the zigzag movements of uncertain philosophic pursuits. It is, therefore, prescribed that whatever be our station in life or calling, we must whole-heartedly apply ourselves to the tasks and the day-to-day chores with utmost care in every detail. The idleness and purposeless activity that is in evidence in the world in the name of art, extravagant rituals, religious tomfoolery of the multifarious creeds, the buffoonery of the priests, narrow personal cults, warring denominations etc. , can all be avoided. Excellence lies in our making use of all the facilities for adding to the wealth and well-being of people. Even small innocent acts like watering a plant, feeding a cow, cleaning a place etc. bring real benefit. Thus, actions are the true test of the progress we make, whether they are noticed or not. The motivation should not depend on the attention or approbation they get from others."

THE POSITIVE MAN

The positive man never complains
And sees the light of the matter
In broader perspective and thereby gains
Goodwill and success, sooner than later.
He ignores considerations other than merit
Except when human kindness is paramount;
Religion, caste, colour or creed he'd surmount
For, they put the country at a great discount.
He is duly courteous but not compromising
With consciousness of National culture and honour;
He firmly believes in universal well-being
And not in a fanatical and individualistic banner.
He exhibits profound scientific temperament
And cares for children's character and development

For, this is the panacea, miraculously potent
In solving every National predicament.
He is thus positive, persevering and pleasant
And always Magnanimous, Action-oriented and Non-violent !

– *Muchimilli*

THE MUSE

The winds from afar have whispered into my ears
The wisdom of the ages that does credit to the sages;
Am I to keep it as though in a cave
And carry it along into my grave?
I burst into a verse and pleaded for a place
But the poets kept me away in disgrace;
'your rhyme is wrong and style is slack
Let your thoughts be bright or bleak.'
I gathered my words and chose my rhyme
Only it beggared my thought sublime;
Naïve and longing I keep it in wait
To commune readily with Thee in delight.
All expression is imperfect whether in philosophy or art,
Though some works are nearer truth aimed at the absolute;
But experience is paramount and plays its vital part
Lasting a life, while knowledge alters and is mute.
Burden my song with the sweetness of your soul
And rear it like a full-blown flower,
For posterity to reep the fruit thereof
And taste of joy in everlasting peace.
My song shall spread over vales and hills
Breathing in full the virgin's grace;
May the muses envy my voice
That all the worlds may rejoice.

– *Muchimilli*

4

Religious Practices, Beliefs and Exploitation

Religious Practices

The earliest reported Dharmic or purificatory fasting was by Ranti Deva, the ancestor of Lord Rama, who fasted for 48 days in a spirit of atonement. His sole life principle was giving relief to the suffering people (*artinasanam*). Jesus was also reported to have fasted for 40 days. Muslims observe the Ramazan type of fast for a month. Gandhiji's Sathyagraha principle is well-known. Ayyappa Devotees follow some austerities for 40 days. They carry rice, ghee and coconuts on their heads and tread long distances. All such practices have to be directed towards purposeful public service apart from the spiritual merit one may acquire in the process. Our religious leaders observe "Chaturmasya". This is an age-old practice. Such observances do immense good. Patience and self-control are promoted by them.

It is, however, possible and also necessary to divert the practices towards promoting the welfare of the society not only by refraining from harmful activities and habits but also by positive engagement in beneficial programmes. Miserliness is eating into the vitals of our society. To get a little help from even 'near and dear' to assist a deserving person is becoming difficult. Sharing of wealth should be made an annual spiritual practice. Worthy people are hard hit by the selfish lot in our society. "Lobhaschet agunena kim Pisunata yadyasti kim patakaih"- Bhartruhari, which briefly means "Niggardliness negates or nullifies all virtues."

If certain images, symbols, chantings, postures etc., are found to be useful in the pursuit of spiritual discipline and excellence, they may be accepted. The innocent, pure and harmless joy in worship is experienced by children and devotees alike. Experiments revealed that certain forms, subjective and objective, produce concentration and calmness of mind leading to enlightenment and bliss. Cynical superstitions and idle predictions of astrology have no place if there is genuine faith. Shrines, temples, masjids and all places of worship should be accessible to all the children of God or human beings subject to certain hygienic and physical regulations. This will surely bring about a change in the attitudes and make people feel that they are one in the eyes of the Supreme. Values like humility, commonness and fellow-feeling are at the background of the regulations sought to be imposed on devotees visiting the places of worship. No one should feel unduly important at least before the Almighty.

Modern minds could find many specious arguments for any cause irrespective of its nobility or worthiness. At the same time, it is gratifying to find that modern science has also developed techniques to verify the justification for certain religious practices and faiths hitherto sustained by belief, intuition and custom. The Cow has been given a place even above human beings and equated to one's mother in the sentiment of Hindu mind from time immemorial. The spirit is a subtle phenomenon which cannot be tested by ordinary physical laws. We are now convinced of the existence of such phenomena as extra-sensory Perception, radiations etc. The ethos of a society is so complex that its special characteristics built into it by several generations of enlightened men cannot be nullified by a gross and materialistic mind. Fully evolved human beings credited with divine perception, saintly people before whose intellectual and spiritual eminence mortal mundane minds were subdued, gave certain norms for the guidance and benefit of humanity. We will do well to respect them and not be corrupted by short-sighted ideas for petty gain.

Blind Beliefs and Superstitions

Superstitions of every imaginable kind have come to stay in our society. In the Dark Ages, some originated out of helplessness and ignorance. A fatalistic attitude was prevalent. All these are contrary to the real spiritual injunction of faith in the Supreme and in oneself. Sometimes what started as a jest became a vain and vested interest harping on the gullibility of the ignorant masses. Thus evolved an enormous body of superstitious practices and beliefs ruining the self-confidence of everyone concerned . Numerology, astrology, palmistry etc, have all been designed to capture the weak and imbecile minds in the net of uncertainty, inaction and negative thinking. They provide a haven to the idle and weak minds seeking excuses and alibis. The true spiritual requirement is only dedication to duty with an invocation for the love of God. Many superstitions perpetrated by even the educated people have dampened and killed the spirit of enterprise in the nation. They have built cowardice into the subconscious mind of people. Most of the religious leaders are failing in their duty by not analyzing the huge body of superstitious practices and beliefs in the modern context on scientific lines while preserving the spirit of religion which is nothing but the love of God and humanity as a whole. A radical change needs to be initiated into the lives of people to discard the cumbersome practices and negative thinking associated with spirituality and religion. The money, time and energy should be directed towards promoting cleanliness, healthy habits and fellow-feeling.

Commercial Exploitation of Religious Sentiments

Principles like hygiene, decency, equality, safety, peace etc., should inform all religious practices. The priest class should be persuaded not to perpetrate the mental stagnation which has become synonymous with religious authority because no one can question the tenets howsoever absurd they may be. A religious council may have to be constituted for this purpose. Further, majority of our children are still subjected to the colonial system of education where they learn very little of our national values or culture; seeds of foreign origin are sown in their tender minds which, as they grow, estrange them from vital national feeling. This is perpetrated by a misreading of Constitutional provisions. Schools and Colleges are not monasteries or nunneries of the minorities. Sinking our foreign-biased religious loyalities, we should opt for national education which will foster true love for our Motherland from childhood itself which is the surest guarantee for integration. Verily, childhood is the key to nationhood.

We now find a wonderful spectacle of Swamis, Priests and Religious Preachers of all sorts with a funny range of dresses, caps, headgears etc., trumpeting the narrow and selfish doctrines as understood by them and passing off as leaders of religious thought. The number and variety of Yoga schools and other religious institutions which sprung into existence all over the world have commercialized the noble pursuit of spirituality. People are misled by the vested interests, sale shops and self-appointed spiritual pedlars. Basically, a person would believe in the beneficial effects of being good and aspires to acquire enduring happiness. There is some strange thirst which seeks fulfilment. Worldly prosperity, sense of atonement, desire for perpetuation, provision for posterity as also the urge to understand, are some of the reasons for this spiritual pursuit which is exploited by the pseudo-priest. This is a vicious circle. Ignorance gets buttressed in the process. The praise of people creates illusion in the thinking and demeanour of the priests that they are genuinely learned. They will overreach themselves and overawe the gullible.

Many great religious leaders spoke little, advised reticence and advocated service. But those who are reaping the benefits and living under the banners are waxing eloquent, giving their separate versions, interpretations etc. Clouds of smoke are created continually, of varying thickness and size! Sycophants and biographers are also concocting myths galore beyond the wildest imagination of the original persons. As Sankara stated, many adopt it as a means for earning livelihood or comforts without any real service to the people. Exceptions are few and far between. In every field we are plagued by redundancy and duplication. We should concentrate on the grains leaving out the haystacks.

Exploitation of the Weak and Poor

Exploitation is rampant in the present society, which is mean and parasitical, killing the very root of goodness and growth. Most of the systems are not related to the production of wealth in the world which can be shared universally. This globe of ours can now be seen as one unit containing various resources of minerals, water, vegetation etc. which can be harnessed in totality. We may take the example of the iron-ore which can be converted into ships, irrigation equipments, construction materials, automobiles and such other progressive means as also into war tanks, bombshells, guillotines, swords etc. Why should it be forever a matter of imagination only that all swords be converted into plough shares or all tanks into tractors! Poverty and suffering can be alleviated, if not eradicated, by global efforts of understanding and love amongst the people. Governments should not promote the vested interests and barriers detracting from this divine design of one human family on this small globe of ours. "The meek shall inherit the Earth". Can this happen if we believe that people will kill each other with sticks, if we don't provide them with arms? Unless we change, the world cannot change. J. Krishnamurti once said (Questions & Answers:) "Most of us find it difficult to change, to give up smoking, for example.... .So, one's responsibility is to bring about a radical change in oneself, because one is the rest of humanity".

At national, state and other lesser levels also, people should realize the great harm that is being perpetuated by this evil of exploitation to the detriment of common good. On every issue, serious thought should be bestowed and intense efforts should be made to remove the scope for exploitation. Resources are being wasted on luxury, pomp, aggrandizement and unproductive paraphernalia in public and private lives.

A simple example may illustrate the need for a new drive. We are entering into the computer age. Whereas the facilities for training provided by the government are meager, private bodies mushroomed all over and are charging exorbitant fees without any standards all over the country which is a typical case of exploitation. The requirement of helmets for two-wheelers was also seen as a case of silly exploitation when more important things are remaining unsolved. In every field, middlemen find a paradise if proper policies are not formulated and implemented with public good as the only criterion. The supreme and simple test laid down by Gandhiji was that whatever is planned or done should be judged with reference to the good it will do to the poorest man in the country. Applying this noble test we should hang our heads in shame at the monumental lavishness in the lifestyles and public spendings if they do not result in benefiting the poor people directly in the first place. Even Fine Arts may be taken to the people. Tyagaraja sang in the streets!

Effective Utilisation of Religious Places for Common Good

The very fact that admission is denied to a human being into a place of worship proves the narrowness of the faith. A place of God or Almighty should be open to all human beings alike as we are all children alike in a spiritual sense. A Shrine, Mosque or Church or whatever be the formal name or attributes of the place with the representation of the Almighty as conceived therein, should be open to all human beings.

By imaginative and enlightened programmes Temples can be made the centres for promotion of selflessness (Nishkama Karma) and self-realization (Aparokshanubhuti). The staff (Archakas and others) in the administration of temples should be Believers (Asthikas) in order to maintain the sanctity of the shrines. They should be educated in the basic norms of divinity and worship. If they are casual and indifferent, the faith of the people gets affected. No efforts should be spared to maintain high standards of cleanliness in and around the temple precincts. Facilities for bathing, feeding, medical treatment etc. should be properly arranged without causing pollution. Provision to educate the visitors and devotees has to be made. The temple staff should wear proper clothing appropriate to their services. The sanctum should be kept clear of ordinary non-Archaka staff. Their presence detracts from the serenity of the place.

It is time that temples are thrown open to all human beings subject only to certain physical and hygienic regulations. Temple administration should also care for the health, education and well-being of the poor and needy as enjoined. People are the body of God. The vast temple areas have to be put to constructive use in the service of the people.

THOUGHTS FOR MEDITATION

Light is joy;
I am in the light;
The light is in me;
I am the light;

I love all people;
That love is Brahman;
I an the Brahman.

Anger is immaturity;
A worthy person shows no anger;
I shall never feel angry;
I am a worthy person;

Good people depend on God alone;
I can easily be of help to some people;
God helps me in becoming good!

My nature is love;
My religion is Service;
My strength is Truth;
My Philosophy is peace.

– *Muchimilli*

5

Gandhian Philosophy

Gandhian Philosophy

The Gandhian Principles of Self-reliance and Non-violence are becoming more and more relevant today. In many foreign countries Gandhian thought is acclaimed as the greatest philosophy of life, political as well as private, to be followed by governments and individuals. In fact, in the United States they have opened departments in every university and educational institution to teach Gandhian principles. It is time we opened our eyes to the practical benefits that the country would derive by adopting the Gandhian way. The late Pandit Nehru had stated "Gandhi was like a beam of light that pierced the darkness and removed the scales from our eyes". No cloud or swarm of insects could eclipse the sun that was Gandhi. He showed that by simple and unilateral means universal results can be achieved. The common people and the poor may not be in a position to practise the virtues strictly. But the rulers, administrators and politicians at least, who are true to Gandhian legacy, should implement the principles in their own lives to inspire others at every level. This is the surest way to bring peace and happiness to all the people in our country.

In a free country, after decades of Independence, one would expect may more improvements in social conditions and attitudes in keeping with the Gandhian thought which is accepted as the foundation of our polity. Otherwise, it is Tweedledum Tweedledee. It calls for bold refinement in the attitude of the educators, administrators and politicians. The common people though credited as the backbone for the preservation of our culture, cannot make all the freedom-dreams come true because it is difficult, if not impossible, to practise certain virtues while living in poverty which is the lot of the majority of our population. The lavishness, luxury, idleness, status-consciousness, selfishness and waste should be curbed by conscious efforts by the powers that be in every field to inspire the common people. The jocular definition that 'a politician is a person who sacrifices your life for his country' can be applied *mutatis mutandis* to other professions also. We have to ward off the evil propensities, purposeless activities, idle disposition and selfish engagements in every walk of life. The refinement can be termed as 'enlightened self-interest' which alone can take us towards the national objectives set forth in our Constitution.

Trusteeship of Wealth

Karl Marx condemned the rich by saying that "all property is theft" whereas Gandhiji has given the true purpose or meaning to life when he said "All property is trust". If this noble idea is understood and sincerely implemented throughout the world it would certainly be possible to transform whole societies and make them live like happy families.

"Seek Knowledge from cradle to the grave" exhorted prophet Mohammad, which is a far cry from fanaticism. "Give away all you have and follow me", demanded Jesus Christ. In the face of the Commandment "Do not kill", Nations are armed to the teeth spending Billions with the capability of eradicating the entire human race from the face of the Earth. Mahatma Gandhi had emphasised the concept of Trust. Thus, the main principles of duty that can save the world to-day can be simplified into a Binary formula of pursuit of knowledge and trusteeship of wealth. Further to the above concept of duty in our living, one may also quote the great Nobel Laureate Mother Teresa Who has concluded after decades of public life "A woman cannot have a better place than the house. The greatest gift is to be a mother and a dutiful wife". It is declared in Gita that the doctrine of duty is very subtle to understand and guidance has to be taken from 'enlightened souls' like Mother Teresa and others as quoted above. The craving to acquire fanciful imported electronic appliances and other expensive gadgets for mere stylish or purposeless living has to be restrained. Some rich persons have the madness to acquire more and more wealth secretively for the benefit of several succeeding generations of their families. This is the greed which causes harm to the progress of the soul and they get condemned in the eyes of Lord. Jesus, therfore, declared "It is easier for a camel to enter the eye of a needle than for a rich man to enter into the Kingdom of God". Every person has to work out his destiny and earn merit in life. In most of the well-to-do families the opportunity to develop spiritually is denied to the children by the pampering and doting of the elders as they are provided with excessive comforts etc. Most of the youngsters so brought up get the snobbery ingrained in them which will lead to dehumanisation in spite of material well-being. Vices and virtues have the peculiar character of self-propulsion after the initial introduction. That is why the elders should take extra care in inculcating human values in the youngsters from very early age.

The training Gandhiji gave to the politicians in the good old days wore off soon after Independence with the result that the concepts of trusteeship of wealth and dedication to duty carry little or no conviction with the so-called elite as general rule. Their main concern was to enjoy the political comforts and amass wealth. There was eagerness all around to occupy huge buildings and palaces for their personal residence whether justified or not. In fact those big buildings should have been turned into schools and institutions to serve the poor. The need is to start a network of schools and institutions which will vigorously propagate and instil into the minds of the children the real and enduring human values and vocational attitudes. We have to pool up all our resources and create the infrastructure for such growth. The lack of proper facilities in the schools and colleges all over the country is lamentable while there is so much lavishness and luxury exhibited in the living styles of our democratic rulers and other elite. Had Gandhiji been alive today he would have given utmost attention to this aspect of our society. He would have seen to it that in every locality there are school buildings and vocational training institutes with all the necessary paraphernalia. If we could not construct the buildings in all places, at least a re-allocation can be made of the existing palatial buildings occupied by the bigwigs or the other neo-rich class of people. That is why there is a great need to propagate the Gandhian principle of trusteeship of wealth and make the present day Gandhians at least live up to the causes of national education and self-reliance.

Karma Theory and Performance of Duties

Reincarnation or transmigration of the soul has been accepted as a vital ingredient of Hinduism. It had also been believed by the Greek philosphers-Socrates, Pythogaras and Plato. Though the Gospel had also referred to it, e.g. Mathew 17-9-13, the Church slowly turned against the idea. Emperor Justinian banned the preaching of it in 533 A.D. and the great Italian philosopher Giordano Bruno was burnt at the stake for doing so. The theory was accepted by the great thinkers. Voltaire, Benjamin Franklin, John Adams, Jefferson, Napoleon, Goethe, Emerson, Whitman, Thoreau, Dickens, Tolstoy, Belzac, Paul Gaugin, Henry Ford, James Joyce, Carl Jung, Erikson, John Mansfield and many others have affirmed it. Immanuel Kant had also finally accepted it in his Critique of Practical Reason. The Karma Theory is closely linked with this.

The Karma theory explains the mystery of people being born into different situations with varied faculties and capabilities. The happenings in life, its vicissitudes, hopes, longings and fulfilments are inexplicable and defy rationalisation beyond a point. The main tenet of Hinduism enjoins on everyone-"Do your duty without undue concern for the fruits thereof". This provides a firm basis for the progress of individual towards realisation or liberation in one span of life or several resultant lives in appropriate circumstances.

Anonymity is the Nature of Reality

Throughout human history, millions of thinkers in all lands attempted to grasp the significance of creation and life. The myriad forms, complexities, variations, pleasures and potentialities have kindled their imagination. The sheer exuberance of the thought of discovery gave them a sort of childish exultation. "Eureka!" It evokes a transcendental sense of wonder to reflect on the limitlessness of events, experiences, phenomena and sensibilities lying between what can be termed as absolute non-existence and absolute existence. We all see that things change and nothing really is permanent. But the wonder of wonders is our total identification with our ego, body and possessions. Even around the great leaders (Religious, Social, Political etc) this self-glorification has come to stay with the result that mankind is divided horizontally and vertically. Nobody pauses to think how absurd it is to attribute infallibility and eternity to the embodied persons who like human beings lived and died. If at all, we may perpetuate their memory by identifying the universal nature of their life and values like love, compassion, service, dedication to do good, promote happiress, etc. Instead, we quarrel and create differences based on the physical identity. In all spheres of human activity we find that these vested interests are multiplying, resulting in conflicts, commercialisation and fanaticism. So much fanfare is created over utterly unimportant issues like disposal of dead bodies and even the ashes. In truth, death dissolves all separateness and demonstrates the oneness of physical existence. It should serve to make us understand the meaning of eternal life which is open to all irrespective of birth, colour, creed, sex, position, wealth etc. In our pettiness and selfishness we try to perpetuate the little ego while anonymity is the nature of Reality.

Some service might have been rendered by several small persons, but then we should have a national approach of universal appeal. It is ridiculous to attempt to preserve burnt bulbs. At this rate the world will be full of petty memorials and graveyards. No headway can be made if an arrow is shot in the reverse with feathers put in the lead. We should subordinate the petty and local interests to certain higher and eternal truths. This lesson is taught by the saint poet, Tulsidas, in his immortal song "Data Ek Raam-Bhikarni Sari Duniya" which means that the only giver is the Lord and all others are beggars of different degrees! Similarly, truth is one, the rest are all zeros. Anonymity appears to be the nature of the ultimate reality. True spiritual life consists in canvassing for this principle so that the littering of world with relics of inconsequential mortals is minimised and the grandeur of the eternal is established.

Involve Common People for Universal Progress

It is important to involve the common people in this universal progress. Leaving the details, for the purpose of the present book, we can only say that people should be made the beneficiaries and not mere spectators of the results achieved. To give an example:- With the sacrifices made by millions we have won freedom; the huge palaces and buildings of erstwhile rulers have been converted into museums, starhotels, Rajbhavans, Rashtrapathi Bhavan, etc. They are now occupied by the leaders and their vast security personnel who give them protection as they cannot live like ordinary people. The fanfare and paraphernalia associated with the palatial buildings could not be given up! People can see them but they cannot use them! The real freedom is in their own home and lives. Therefore the spiritual purport is entirely different from the unfeeling and lifeless structures. Had Gandhi been alive he would have insisted on using the spacious buildings for schools, colleges, hospitals and such public causes which are direly in need. People would also love such transformation in the use of the colonial constructions. Otherwise, it is Tweedledum Tweedledee!

Benefit of the Poorest to be the Aim

Asceticism, abstinence and self-denial are much misunderstood and equated to poverty. Mahaveer (470 B.C), the Founder of Jainism had propounded "not to own any property" as one of the five vows. Buddha denied himself the Kingdom and the pleasures. Vivekananda, when offered the comfort of a bed in Amercia, wept and rolled on the floor thinking of the miserable conditions of the people in India. Gandhiji's simplicity is wellknown. Ho-chi-Minh of Vietnam did not wear Chappals saying that all of his countrymen were first to be so provided. Jesus ordained *"Sell all that thou hast and give to the poor and follow me"*. This is different from the poverty suffered by many great men. Rt. Hon'ble Srinivasa Sastry was known as "shirtless sastri" and his mother refused mangoes for inability to buy salt to pickle them! Dr. Radhakrishnan, J. Krishnamurthy (Theosophical Society), Lal Bahadur Sastri and many others tasted dire poverty. Gandhiji wanted to prepare the people for the freedom struggle and prescribed simple life as a norm. This was soon forgotten after Independence by most of his own followers. But Gandhiji was not against progress as a free Nation, which includes modernisation, industrialisation, high-tech multi-revolution etc. If properly understood, Gandhism is not opposed to modern living, ergonomics, modern medicines and other advanced ways of public and private life. His emphasis was on service to the people and eradication of poverty which are basic to Hinduism. In his own words Gandhiji was a "Practical Idealist".

The Quality and Purpose of Life

Intuitive wisdom, divine revelation, unerring ratiocination, incisive intellectual analysis and comprehension, the deepest perception of the greatest of minds throughout history, have all laid down that one and only purpose of human life is to make the world a better, healthier, happier and more beautiful place to live in. All exertions, activities, knowledge, science, inventions and every conceivable application of life-force should be oriented towards this. In this context, it is worthwhile to note that the time spent by every human being can easily be analysed and harnessed to better purpose. For example, the habit of smoking is an obnoxious thing which is indulged in most thoughtlessly on ever-widening scale, resulting in pollution, accidents and ill-health. Many are deluded by false notions of tension, relief, enjoyment and freedom. The supreme and simplest way to instil discipline is to propagate relentlessly the value and purpose of human life. Religion played a vital role in this regard. This has prompted even the greatest rationalist like Voltaire to proclaim that even if there is no God, there is need to invent one. If a person is God-fearing, it will ensure an awareness from within, of the need to conform to certain standards of behaviour and purification within and without.

The Present Century is characterised as one of Anxiety and the previous three as of Progress, Reason and Enlightenment. Let us imagine the 21st Century to be one of Peace. The unprecedented Social Changes and the tremendous advancement in Science and Technology have brought in their wake increased emotional stress and strain in the modern man. The conservative cultural values and systems are being questioned. The spate of institutions added to complexities and tensions. All these result in emotional disturbances as also social conflicts. Man, however, learns to adjust himself and make compromises in the process. It is not generally realised that the quality of life has deteriorated. Many psychiatric syndromes, psychosomatic disorders, anxiety neurosis, alienation, ambivalence and certain compulsive habits have increased. This may be imperceptible because no serious study has been made as to why, we as a nation with tremendous potential, known for resourcefulness and wisdom, are still poor among the poorest. In simple words, India is a rich country but with poor people now. Of course, we are now steadily on the path to progress.

Innate Mysteries of Life

Even ordinary experiences through our faculties or senses can be revealing of innate mystery of life. Think of the simple question-why is sugar sweet? Many such innocent inquiries defy explanation in the ordinary sense. One may even brush them aside as idle curiosity or childish prattle. Great scientists including Einstein, Raman and others, have accepted that true scientific analysis gives rise to metaphysical thoughts. A sincere mind will find the progression as atheist, agnostic and theist. The ultimate explanation is easily given as the unknown or the Supreme having designed the world of experiences to be so. In this view, the answer to the question why is sugar sweet-may simply be given as "because God has made it so". All explanations, reasoning etc. cannot but result in such safe summing up. The innumerable imponderables are stepping stones for the wise as they are stumbling blocks for the ignorant. Again, there are pitfalls in blindly following this divine dispensation. Fatalism is as bad as fanaticism. What is the place for human will and effort in the scheme of things? We should not take ourselves to be mere sheep or unintelligent beings or sinners only fit to be driven and consumed in this cauldron of life and death. We are a highly evolved species.

Righteousness

'Hunger and thirst' for righteousness was the main theme of great lives. It was the sole purpose of the saints. Valmiki, and Sankara stand out amongst them. Ramanuja, Madhva and Vallabha followed. The Alwars, Nayanmars, the religious poets and saints in all languages expressed their experiences and understanding in this noble pursuit and gave some guidelines. Namdev, Narsi Mehta, Vallalar, Tulasi, Pothana, Valluvar, Kamban, Vallathol & many others gave their exposition in their own idiom but the message is the same. Many had bodily sufferings e.g. Dayanand, Ramakrishma Paramahamsa, Ramana Maharashi whereas Vallalar, Tukaram, Thyagaraja and many others had easy deliverance from the mortal coil. Sant Jnaneswar, Ramatheertha, Vivekananda, Vinobha Bhave and many others gave up their lives. Self-immolation was resorted to by some of them. Peaceful life, easy death and reaching God's abode are prayed for by all Hindus. Euthanasia may not be opposed to the Hindu spirit.

Discipline

Sri Maha Bhagavatam, Maha Bhakta Vijayam, Tirukkural, Divya Prabandham, Periya Puranam of Sekkizhaar, Thriruvachakam of Manickkavachakar, Joti Agaval and Arutpa of Vallalar and similar such spiritual accounts of great devotees would drive home to us the important principle that the divinely evolved souls should be allowed to live according to their own liking or disposition though they may not conform to normal or acceptable patterns. Some of the saints suffered from a high libido, e.g. Jaya Dev, Tulasi Das. Chaitanya Mahaprabhu was twice married, but developed God-intoxication. Some evolved out of other vices like miserliness (Tukaram). Ramakrishna Parmahamsa and Gandhiji can be compared in their great continence. Vivekananda once sat on a hot stove to punish himself for lack of mental control over an evil thought. It is, therefore, necessary for ordinary mortals to cultivate discipline. The Jains observe *Paryushan Parva* with five main duties including fasting, visiting temples etc. The requirements are simple indeed. Hinduism respects learning and dedication to duty. Women, children and elders are to be treated with consideration. Nowadays, we find growing indifference towards elders and indulgence in self-destructive habits like smoking. The social environment and frustration are responsible for this. We have to build up a Defence Mechanism to protect the mental health of people.

The commentary of Adi Sankara on Brahma Sutras outlines four pre-requisites called "Sadhana Chatustaya" to qualify for engaging in the analysis of Brahman or the Supreme which may be described as (i) discrimination between permanent and transitory (ii) detachment from the fruits of action (iii) discipline of body and mind (iv) devotion or urge for liberation. Sage Vasista also traverses at great length in the classic work *"Yogavasista"* what is called *"Astangayoga"* or the eight fold path of Yoga dealing with the discipline of the body and mind. Suffice it to say that 'Fairness of mind' is at the root of all these exercises.

Sacrifice-the Soul of Success

Sacrifice is given the pride of place. The essence of human birth lies in the exertion to contribute to the quality of life in and around. Selfish living negates its very nature. Man as the beneficiary of the entire creation around him should prove himself worthy of it. Here lies the secret. True joy can be experienced in repaying this debt of nature as it were. A rational understanding would limit the requirement of rendering service primarily to the needs of man. In other words, it is the prerogative of man to harness nature for his benefit. If all the available idle time is employed towards creation of the necessary infrastructure for civilised living, the country can be transformed. This may call for a sacrifice in the form of say, Shramadan or contribution of labour. Giving away vast tracts of barren land under the Bhoodan Movement as donation would not help the growth of agriculture unless the inputs are forthcoming Similarly, mere charity will not eradicate beggary.

For the affluent sections of the society, the idea of trusteeship should be brought home as Mahatma Gandhi had striven in recent times. The joy in giving and sharing of the benefits of birth and acquisition has to be experienced to be believed. Buddha and Gandhi can be taken to be representing this ideal of sacrifice. But, for ordinary mortals, it is laid down that they should not neglect their own well-being. At the same time, it is open to them to make true happiness a part of the worldly life by making the spirit of sacrifice a guiding principle. The quotations of the highest authority from the Veda and Gita are (i) Tyagenikena Amrutatwa Manasuh; (ii) Tyagat Shantiranantarm; Asantasya Kutassukham. The little ego of the individual plays havoc with his mind preventing him from realising the truth and experiencing this happiness. The superior man constantly reflects on the impermanence of things and relations but ceaselessly works as an instrument of progress for adding to the quality of life in and around. This supreme happiness can be realised even in small acts in life.

Sacrifice is also involved in the act of limiting one's requirements or sparing to others what is in excess of one's needs. As Gandhiji put it, there is enough for everybody's need in the world but not enough even for one man's greed. The tendency to amass fortunes for generations to come is harmful. Heritage lies in allowing people to grow by their own efforts and self-development. After creating a minimum base as it were, one must radiate and become benevolent. Like little drops of water making a mighty ocean, this disposition will herald a new era. In this peculiar chess game of life, we can push ourselves to the different positions though there seems to be some divine or inscrutable corroboration in the process. The knowledge of mortality as contrasted with the absence of it in animals gives this special status and capability to man.

Thus, the unique privilege of human birth should not be wasted in pettiness and selfish pursuits without contributing to the well-being of society and the quality of life which are implied in the concept of sacrifice. Interestingly, if it is thought that happiness results from the identification of the self with a single person or body, it greatly increases with the expansion of this identity to cover a larger body of people, the ultimate being the love of mankind as a whole. Selflessness is tested with reference to people with whom there is no blood or emotional relationship. It should not be with strings or expectations. It should be in a spirit of glorification of the supreme human quality which is inherent. With a little effort and will, one can experience this true happiness.

By treating everything as evanescent, man gets prepared to sacrifice. The value was reflected in actual life. If one's marriage was decided by the elders, it was accepted. If the widow was not allowed to remarry she obeyed it so that some other poor girl may get the chance to marry. The entire fabric of society was based on the spirit of sacrifice. The entire fabric of society was based on the spirit of sacrifice. Motherhood is thus symbolised and venerated which is natural and the mother is given the pride of place in Hinduism. They laid great stress on the pre-natal care because it influenced the child to be born. A good society depended so much on the birth of good children. Marriage was not a carnal affair but was conceived in the context of building up a society with good human beings.

Life is beautiful, Life is divine
It's truly sublime for those without 'mine and thine'!
You've become united in such life as 'wife and husband'
To prosper and rejoice and to fulfill the joyous command
Of rishis, your forbears and gods in unison
To enrich mankind with universal love and compassion.
Dubts, differences and difficulties shall vanish as mist
And divinity, dutifulness and cheer shall ever exist
With warmth in your midst so that the Heavens are pleased,
To bless the Mother Earth and her enduring seed!
May you thus be blessed in all that you devoutly wish,
Act and achieve that posterity will acclaim and cherish!

– *Muchimilli*

At every stage the element of sacrifice for the happiness of others is built in. Prarabdha is destiny which is responsible for the possessions and endowments but Purushardha is freewill by which we can build up the future. This conflict is reconciled and the motivation provided for pursuing a life of righteousness. Modern living and the onslaught of western education upset these values fundamental to the Vedic thought of Hinduism. Crass utilitarianism and individualism are now rampant. We have to instil with a sense of urgency the values of Hinduism into our society again. This will be the greatest service to mankind in the cause of peace.

Even well-to-do people do everything possible to make more money for greater comforts and selfish ends. They seldom seek to help deserving persons by providing them opportunities for self-development. Their stupid philosophy is usually expressed thus: "One must suffer and try to come up on his own. Even gold should pass through fire". This has disheartened and ruined many an young man of promise while worthless people are pampered with ill-gotten wealth. God's trust is betrayed by the rich people as a general rule. There are no doubt exceptions who alone are really saving our country from utter ruin. It is pertinent to mention here about the beautiful poems of Abou Ben Adam by Leigh Hunt and Peace & Plenty by Muchimilli. Good people don't work with fanfare. But their efforts are negligible as compared to the large-scale degradation, destruction and even dehumanisation suffered by good people. The Lord works through human form Daivam Manusha Rupena. When people on whom fortune has smiled even as political and economic upstarts get carried away to become "Selfish Pigs" (see Bhartruhari) then the county is doomed. That is why Hinduism exhorts the wealthy to remember that death is lurking or inevitable and their good deeds alone count in this as also in afterlife. For the poor, however, there is the protection of """Apatdharma" even if they lapse from virtue. India will regain its glory only if the wealthy or well-placed people realise their responsibility to God in improving the quality of life by giving a helping hand to good persons who can be easily identified by mere human instinct. This basic resolution will itself show the way for the sincere people. It is so thrilling to engage oneself in this task. This is the real joy of life.

A little reflection on our way of living generally reveals selfishness and ego as prime motivators behind our actions, however highly placed one might be. The poor and the illiterate have to struggle very hard to make a living and it is too much to expect them to make any sacrifices. In fact they feel resigned to their fate. Their weakness and humility are a part of their helplessness which is easily exploited without compunction. This is the stark truth everywhere, the realisation of which alone can improve the situation universally. The meaning of the Vedic utterence "Tena Tyaktena Bhunjita" has not been properly realised to this day except to some extent by Gandhiji who stated "All property is trust."

The negative aspect of the above maxim viz. "Do not covet other's Property" is given undue prominence. The fallacy is that rich people assume vested interest or identity with their possessions, which takes the form of greed, avarice and dog-in-the-manger attitude towards society as a whole. This is destructive of harmony and peace. There is total estrangement from the spirit of sacrifice which flows form the law of love. Sacrifice is different from mere patronage, favours or charity. We owe it to ourselves as a duty. "The giver is twice blessed than the receiver" is a significant statement.

Importance of Courage

Courage is the basis for progress. Sankara described the dumb as the person who cannot speak up good advice (KoMookah?). Bharturhari condemned the lack of receptivity to good words (Jeernamangey). Similarly, Confucius lamented lack of their implementation. Many a western genius lived a miserable life but did not give up courage e.g. Newton, Galelio, Descartes, Copernicus, Kepler, Cavendish. Alfred Nobel remained unmarried and lived a miserable life. Of course, we are honouring the NobleLaureates with the fund left by him. Jesus was crucified. Gandhiji was persecuted. It is found that goodness is discouraged and even ridiculed with the result that its very existence is at stake. An attitudinal change is needed. Tolerance is not meekly making up with mindless fanatical elements pampered by false prophets. Don't we accept the fantasy of Rupee coin proclaiming "Save me and I shall save you."! The same is eternally true of Dharma also (Dharmo Rakshati Rakshitah).

The Pledge

Hinduism owed its true character to Lord Rama who integrated the entire country wielding his powerful bow known as Kodandam and exhibiting his sterling qualities and valour. Gandhiji's strong armoury consisted of the bow-like Charka which is horizontally laid as compared to the vertical *kodandam* of Rama. Wielding the Charka and practising supreme love for the people, with faith in Rama, Gandhiji brought the Nation to work in unison and peace till freedom was achieved. By the touch of Rama's feet the stone melted and become a beautiful woman (Ahalya); Monkeys became warriors. Gandhiji turned dust into men and slavish minds into champions of freedom!

Talent flourished under Gandhiji's patronage and he searched it out with great care and affection as proved by Rajen Babu, Vallabhai, Nehru, Vinobha, Venkatappayya (designer of our National Flag), Rajaji and a host of other workers for the Nation. This noble urge to spot talent and nourish the proper persons has almost disappeared after Independence. The CBI system is geared mainly towards checking monetary corruption leaving out the more dangerous corruption of putting down goodness at every opportunity. We should reverse the outlook or systems which ignore or discredit merit and values. The Vedic approach is strikingly illustrated by example of the Chataka bird which lays its eggs in the upper region of the sky. They hatch as they fall down towards the earth and the fledgelings realise their fall from the supreme heights and make efforts to regain the same with all their might. In olden days people were thus inspired to attain spiritual heights and to become good human beings, worthy of the descent from Heaven. The songs of the saints reflect this ideal. The lamp or the flame always leaps towards the sun into the skies above, whichever way it is held! But alas! with the class bias, people are trying to prove themselves to be more and more backward for getting the benefits. There is a psychic regression in the whole Nation that backwardness is advantageous than pursuit of excellence. This is ruinous to the society and human growth.

The three worlds of Bhu, Bhuah and Suah referred to in the Gayatri Mantra may also be related to the three stages or manifestations of Matter consisting of Matter, Elements etc. Energy consisting of gravity, light, magnetism etc. and Intellect consisting of knowledge, spirit, motivation, values etc. The sole theme of the Mantra, apart from its intrinsic value of metrical structure of spiritual sounds, is to effectuate evolution towards higher states of intellectual life of human beings. If we are true to the Hindu tradition represented by the Gayatri Mantra, we should give full support for merit in every human being and motivate them towards excellence.

Concentration, Meditation and Trance are the three states of mental effort. It is a transition or ascendance from objective to subjective. Senses are used in Concentration, distilled in Meditation and transcended in Trance. The final stage is referred to as super-consciousness. Intuition is its off-shoot. It is full of happiness. It can also be directed to a purpose other than self-relisation. Gandhiji had experimented it for deciding the course of action on several occasions. The saints have used it in describing the nature of divinity in all its aspects. The stamp of super-consciousness is clearly evident when we read the saintly compositions which are beyond the capabilities of ordinary men, howsoever literate they might be. Hinduism has evolved the techniques of sublimating sensory knowledge and intellectual acumen.

Vaanaprasta or Retirement is a well thought out institution of Hinduism relevant to the present times. It will generate employment for new and younger people. Giving pension to employees prevents or dissuades them from seeking further employment. In the present day almost all the retired people seek jobs for want of proper understanding or motivation. This disturbs the social ethos and vitiates peaceful growth of the society. Retired people should as far as possible not seek further employment and hang on to offices. The idea of giving pension was conceived in this context. Those who can afford to live without it should readily seek retirement and enrich the life of the society. There is no dearth of new talent. On the contrary, it will be unexplored and will remain unnoticed, if opportunity is denied by the old people sticking on to their professions and jobs till the last breath. Hinduism has evolved the glorious technique of social growth and individual emancipation.

It is time we opened our eyes to the realities of the Indian situation and revive the values of "Respect for learning" and 'Dedication to duty' to offset the evil growth of sycophancy and abuse of muscle and money power in our society. The social evils can be eliminated only when every person is mentally prepared to make a little sacrifice in the larger interests of the society. In this context the following Pledge is significant:

> "Every able man reared of this soil shall dedicate himself for the human cause, for the glorious cause of the happiness of man and good of the society and it shall ever be my endeavour to make every man so determined if not so able."
>
> – *Muchimilli*

ON RETIREMENT

Friends! Allow me to thank you and tell
My Hearty Greetings of Farewell!
Even if my family and friends disapprove
I had to laydown my office and move!

Breathless businessmen with their wares
Plodding pedestrains with their cares,
People preoccupied with their own welfare
Enter and exit in life's thoroughfare!

But an endearing smile or a word of care
Like a pure lily will the love declare;
Fortunately, I reaped the warmth so rare
From hearts which kindness and nobility bear.

When the burdens of life come at last to pass
And the Balance Sheet is prepared with profit and loss,
Life shall be filled with fragrance and peace
From flowers of friendship and goodness of deeds!

– *Muchimilli*

6

Peace and Happiness

Peace-the Content of Happiness

A critical and comprehensive study of the latest developments in Science and Technology in the varied fields, including Cosmology, Cybernetics, Genetic Engineering, Para-Psychology, Bio-Technology, Lasers, Robotics, Transplantation Surgery, Super-Computer, Super-conductors, Space Odysseys, Nuclear Research, Star-wars etc. would show that the zenith of human glory is within our reach but is eluding us because we have neglected the essential aspect of existence. The culmination of all learning and the pinnacle of human glory consists in the realisation and establishment of peace within and without in the true sense of the word. It implies fulfilment and identification with the supreme and results in a feeling of oneness with mankind as a whole without the barriers of colour, creed, religion, race, caste, language, nationality etc. This is the spiritual essence of life which has been set as the goal for human progress.

Persecution faced by the saints is revealing. The Sermon on the Mount devotes three paras to this aspect and comforts the persecuted with a "Reward in Heaven". In Hindu thought, however, Adi Sankara gave a specific direction to the people to show respect to a Sanyasi even by appearance, without going into his merits. In actual practice also, the Hindu ethos is one of simplicity and reverence towards the saintly people. This is being exploited and commercialised by some persons under different banners. The common platform of spirituality is disappearing and external appearances of several separate types are hardening. Even the manner of wearing the Naamam on the forehead has created differences with bitterness leading to several court cases also. The prejudices have grown with different practices of Sivaites, Vishnavites, Aryasamajists, Buddhists, Jains, Namdharis, Sikhs, Nirankaris, different missions like Ramakrishna, Aurobindo, Sai Baba, Iskcon, Gowdiyamutt, Meher Baba etc. They have all evolved separate insignia for physical identification, symbols, prayers, etc. It is necessary to integrate all these and give importance only to the ultimate principle of Santi or Peace.

The Bhagavadgita and other scriptures of different religions or faiths support the idea of observing the "Peace Fortnight". The Peace Fortnight (Santipaksham) can be observed from 1st to 15th January each year by all people dedicated to peace. The main practices to be observed are (1) to have cheerful disposition and show courtesy to all (2) to forgive and forget all unpleasant things and not to carry them forward; (3) not to cause harm to other by words or deeds; (4) to plant or water a tree; (5) to wear white clothes or a band as insignia on at least one day; (6) to sincerely practise and propagate the norm "Be good; Do good" and (7) not to carry any weapons. A simple prayer is given below;

PEACE PRAYER

"Oh Dear Lord,

You are all-pervading and living in all the beings throughout the world. Bless us to be aware of Thy presence in greater measure. Help us in our work for better and healthier life on this earth. May there be peace and goodwill amongst all individuals and nations. This is my earnest prayer."

A new era of peace, prosperity and happiness to the entire people of the world can be heralded if all the available media for public communication are geared up to this task of spreading the fundamental concept of peace that mankind is one large family and there is no place for arms, hatred war and killings, as indulged in today by militarist cliques or governments for solving the problems faced by them. On the other hand, the easiest and surest way to solve all problems facing the human race today is to adopt the above stated principle of peace which is the essence of the teachings of the Vedic Seers, Christ, Mohammad, Zoraster, Buddha, Mahaveera, Tao, Baha Ullah, Gandhi and other saviours who are all one in spirit, though born at different places and times on this small globe of ours. As worthy beneficiaries of this glorious heritage, let us live up to their expectations and move into the 21st Century as one great family.

"Lord, make me an instrument of your peace
Where there is hatred, let me sow love;
Where there is injury, pardon;
Where there is doubt, faith;
Where there is despair, hope;
Where there is darkness, light,
And where there is sickness, joy.
O Divine Master, grant that I may not
So much seek to be consoled as console;
To be understood as understand;
To be loved as to love.
For, it is in giving that we receive,
It is in pardoning that we are pardoned
And it is in dying
That we are born to eternal life".

It is very easy to quote from the scriptures and other authorities in support of either of the versions regarding any proposition. A coin has two faces, the magnet has two opposite poles and many such examples can be stated for the sake of arguments. But, this is entirely different from the duality of good and evil which is perceived through discrimination. It is also attained by self-analysis. The touchstone of this is Peace. Peace is more important than success. The rule should, therefore, be 'Peace at any cost' and not 'Success at any cost'. Here also there are pitfalls and scope for hypocritical arguments but not difficult to overcome if the conviction is not to do harm to our fellow human beings. No effort should be spared to carry relentlessly this message of "Be good; do good" even against all odds of ridicule and repression. Then only the seeds of the noble civilisation sown by our forbears will regerminate and breaking the overlying soil of selfishness, sprout towards the Heaven of Progress, yielding divine flowers and fruit of friendship and peace, for the eternal well-being of humans on this Earth.

Truth-the Foundation of Peace

The sun truly rose in the East and spread its rays far and wide. The Supreme, true to its nature, is conceived as one, but the paths are many. All are children of God. His love is unbounded. There is no room for enmity, war, hatred, fanaticism and other evils. Several incarnations (Avatars) depict the valour and purpose of the Supreme in vanquishing the evil and protecting the righteous. Their enchanting forms captivate the imagination and give a thrill of joy. An open, pure, honest, innocent or childlike mind, if exposed, without compulsion or inducement, to the symbolism, imagery, worship, emotions, sentiments, fantasy, tenets, pursuits and ideals of the different religions, will naturally accept the freedom, beauty, tolerance, openness, vision and universality of Hinduism. It includes all and excludes none. Moreover, it does not depend for its survival on a single individual, event or book. Monotony leads to stagnation. So the Hindu sages accepted varied perceptions of the Truth. All questions are answered and enquiry is encouraged. This is the challenge.

"The Truth shall make you Free". The four Mahavakyas from the four Veds direct us towards that. To similar effect is the Biblical saying "Be silent and know that I am God" and adds that the Kingdom of God is within! When Abraham

Lincoln wrote in his private diary "I promised my God I would do it" he was indicating the true strength of his being. Thus, from the many Gods who were devised for endowing material benefits, we can turn towards the indwelling light which is truth.

The Mystique of Happiness

First-hand knowledge or understanding of the source of Happiness cannot be had from mere enjoyment of physical comforts or sensuousness. There is a mystique about it. It is found as an a priori or intuitive instinct associated with life itself as part of nature. An instance of this can be found in the fact of the newly born baby or calf locating the source of its nourishment. Particularly in wild life, this assumes great significance as there is no external guidance and death is certain without this instinct. As for human beings, affections are pronounced and the parents take due care. Pursuit of happiness is a strong impulse in man and is even made a fundamental right. In ancient Hindu thought, they have given great importance to this aspect of our existence and made it a duty enjoined upon human beings to work for and realise happiness.

The innermost sheath of life is conceived as consisting of the vibrations of happiness, bliss or beatitude, the outer four sheaths being the nutritional, oxygenous, egoistic and spiritual. Most commonly, our experience of happiness is limited to the gratification of senses of sight, hearing, smell, taste and touch and the relative gross organs of the body viz, the eyes, ears, nose, tongue and skin are employed for the purpose. Further, senses like hunger, fear, sleep, procreation are also common to the animals and the humans. The distinguishing feature of a human being is the sense of discrimination or judgement of good and evil. This gives rise to the idea of motivation in actions. Though, in nature, fulfilment is per-ordained like in the sprouting of a seed, blooming of the flower, the entire animal and plant life appears to be peculiarly limited or conditioned in contrast with the will for self-development available to the human being. The sages of yore probed into the mystery of creation and spent whole lives in unravelling the secrets, for the wellbeing and happiness of mankind. These truths have been borne out by the experiences of the properly initiated persons. The authenticity lies in the fact that they hold good even today and can be verified by one's own experience.

Yoga, Music and Fine Arts have also been acclaimed as sources of happiness. In the ultimate analysis, it is a discovery or an expression of the self. The real foundation of the basic musical notes is analysed to be corresponding to vibration at the different nodes of prana or the life force. Great souls who experienced this joy of liberation through music have testified in no uncertain terms to the unfailing result of the pursuit of perfection through music. It is one bliss or beatitude. It is Nadamrutayoga. Other arts like Painting, Dance, Sculpture etc., have also provided the means for fulfilment of the inner urge of the artists for self expression. It should not be confused with misguided and purposeless activity which is mostly in evidence nowadays. When the ideal or objective is clearly analysed and understood, it would impart refinement, creativity and consummation to the means employed. Commercialistion has corrupted this noble objective and diminished the quality of performance. When the true joy is not experienced by the artists, it cannot be communicated to others. 'Swayam Teernah Paran Taraishyati'.

Knowingly or unknowingly, the activities of life have the ultimate goal of happiness. Delusion distorts and distracts the pursuit of happiness. Significantly, science and technology which are meant to subserve human progress and happiness can do immense harm if they fail to supplement laws and forces of nature and work at cross purposes. The search for truth is different form idle and purposeless curiosity. Once the attainment of happiness is taken as the ultimate objective, it would not lie in mere satisfaction of the appetite of senses as in the case of animals. Education should give us this enlightenment or understanding of the contribution we have to make towards the quality of life within and without. We then have to face the fact duality in every aspect of existence like light-darkness, pain-pleasure, success-failure, health-sickness, and so on. There may be people who would say" I love suffering if I can have the strength to bear it". The complexity and multifariousness of events, physical objects, experiences etc. can be reduced to represent this duality. This phenomenon can be further sublimated to produce the state of happiness which is the summum bonum of life. This is the topmost point of physical life. The greatest of minds throughout human history have been exercised on finding the means to experience and live in this state of happiness and to bring it within the reach of every person.

We have given above the five broad methods of realisation of this state of happiness viz.1) sacrifice, 2) duty 3) prayer 4) knowledge and 5) yoga, Music and fine arts. Forms, modalities, language, colour, creed, manners, scriptures, etc., are all secondary. The essence should not be identified with them. We have come a long way from the beginings of civilisation. Mankind has amassed enormous power in the form of nuclear armaments, other destructive weapons, etc. to destroy itself totally. This is the paradox of our material advancement. The solution lines in canvassing the spiritual message of pursuit of happiness through peace as can be obtained through the five instrumentalities discussed above. The purpose of life should not be limited to the donning of external insignia and growing of certain symptoms or symbols. The success of the present civilization lies in making the above understanding peremptory and universal.

Human happiness is paramount. From the beginnings of civilized societies, every conceivable study, activity and enterprise was directed towards this. Humans organized themselves into groups and in different parts of the world developed separate systems for survival and growth. Commonness was forgotten and selfishness overtook individually and collectively in all the societies. Now at this point of time and evolution over centuries, we can readily grasp the significance of our existence on this small globe of ours and rise above the pettiness and selfishness built into our systems through ignorance. In Nature there is only creativity and love. Man as the highest form of species can easily prove to be an embodiment of this love. All negative qualities of hatred, ill will etc. are the symptoms of ignorance which can be easily dispelled like ages of darkness by a small candle.

JAGADGURU ADI SANKARA

When conscience was dull and knowledge mute
And the very word of Veda lost repute,
When acrimony and chaos with atheistic creeds
Plagued our 'Dharma' like worms and weeds,
Thou hast dawned with reason resplendent
And dispelled the doubt and founded thy judgement;
Oh Lion of vedanta and Lord Incarnate,
With heart, mind and soul to thee I prostrate.

– *Muchimilli*

7

Importance of Learning and Proper Utilisation of Talents

Knowledge is Supreme

Knowledge is Supreme. *"Prajnanam Brahma"* is the vedic utterance. It is the culmination of all action. *"Janane Parisamapyate"* according to Gita. "Seek knowledge from the cradle to the grave", declared prophet Mohammed, which is a far cry from the fanaticism. Poet Milton had postulated that "the end of all learning is to know God", which is above mere 'father and son' relationship. What is then the sum total of learning? The seers have defined it as "Knowing which all else is known". Nothing remains to be known thereafter. This is the secret urge and sole motivation for Einstein to work on his 'Unified Field' theory. The greatest intellectuals from ancient to the modern times have made this pursuit of knowledge their way of life. It can thus be proclaimed as an end in itself. The candle burns out shedding light, so also the sun.

Knowledge associated with happiness is pure and absolute. It is preceded by discrimination, detachment, discipline and dedication. The above four ingredients or qualifications have been elucidated by discerning minds endowed with extraordinary intellectual prowess of whom Sankara is singularly outstanding. Briefly given, the four prerequisites are (i) the ability to distinguish between the permanent and the ephemeral. This gives the ability to see through things and events (ii) Indifference to the enjoyment of the fruits of action. This promotes total objectivity, dispassion and purposefulness (iii) Physical and mental equipment and mastering of the skills. This accounts for thoroughness, equilibrium and proficiency, (iv) Total involvement or commitment towards realisation. This synchronises the mind, body and action and brings about total harmony within and without. Applied knowledge serves the world in promoting the well-being and prosperity of the human race. This is the prime off-shoot of pure knowledge. It is even described as incidental and involuntary like the heat which is concomitant to light. Sages are known to have brought about beneficial events and prosperity to the world by their contemplation in the process of self-realisation. Thus, the sublime knowledge is blissful and is a source of happiness to one and all, materially and spiritually.

True learning alone can provide the necessary direction to human activity in all its phases. This has been given a spiritual status and divinity in ancient thought because its sole aim and purpose was to bring happiness to man in real terms. But many religious bigots and preachers have corrupted the institutions with negative, unproductive or idle theories which militated against active engagement in worldly pursuits that contribute to the wealth and happiness of mankind. Vested interests have been created to sustain generations of misguided followers of these creeds in the name of religion and faith. Enquiry or openness is forbidden to them. Thus, bigotry and priesthood thrive on mutual support and preyed on the gullibility of the followers. Even the highly educated are not immune to the blind conformity with outdated and anachronistic insignia like personal appearance, wearing of caps, beards, etc. on compulsion and not on volition. Thus, there is no evidence of true learning in the present society where the divisions based on vested interest are multiplying day-by-day which is a far cry from the ideal of *"Vasudhaiva Kutumbakam"* or one-world-family propounded by the seers of yore. The integrating factors of true knowledge and dedication to duty in the service of mankind are yielding place to disintegrating factors of fanatical and individualistic banners and vested interests in every walk of life.

The ancient Greek physicians and thinkers can be said to have drawn inspiration from the ancient Indian wisdom which Indians have long since neglected. In Voltaire's words, the Greeks came to India to lisp a little knowledge. Our Scriptures and Upanishads repeatedly exemplify the supreme spirit of work and cooperation in such glorious lines as "Sahanavavatu", "Sanghachhadhvam", "Parasparam Bhavayanatah" etc. The perverted and crooked theories of Kautilya, as propounded true to his name in his Arthasastra, have no relevance now. Sakuni, Machiavelli or Goebbel should not be revived. The colonial doctrine "The King can do no wrong", had once permeated every rung of the bureaucratic setup trampling upon every tender sprout of talent throughout.

Jesus declared that the lamp of knowledge cannot be lighted where the winds of foolishness blow too strong. When power speaks, wisdom has to be silent. The solution lies in replacing the sadistic pleasure of tormenting the learned with the joy of patronishing them in every walk of life. Let us pray for a change of heart. A good heart is worth many heads. We must restore the respect for learning. We should not equate power with knowledge. A person with superior intellect or wisdom is not to be isolated and humiliated. Mediocrity may be ruling the roost. Genius is not to be given the boot. Porcupines and snakes are always feared. The rat race makes mice of men. When one is promoted or recruited as Manager, a declaration and undertaking may be obtained to read "I am and shall always behave like a human being", like the similar declaration in the Vedic mantra "Ahmannado, Aham Annado". Such Managers by whatever name called, can make our Freedom dreams come true.

Misplaced Talents

In the present world, in spite of the democratic systems for electing the best representatives to the legislatures which make the laws for the governance, we find most members do not have the necessary talents and the bureaucratic system continues to dominate and stall the progress. In the present party system there are no enlightened norms for selection of the candidates. Partyless democracy is an ideal that cannot be a achieved easily. Unless we are able to build up a cadre of enlightened representatives and public servants who can look beyond the petty party or other interests, the present muddle will continue. Harmony and peace will recede from the reach of the people. Even in educational, academic, scientific institutions, narrow linguistic, ethnic, caste, class, party, regional and religious considerations dominate. The minds shrink. With the result, the ideals of yoga, which are our proud heritage from the Upanishadic time, will remain a mirage. Thinkers and educated elite should come down heavily on this undesirable aspect of our present system and promote a universal outlook without inhibitions, superstitions or selfish motives. In real terms, we should not select our parliamentarians and public men from amongst old bandicoots, profiteers, unscrupulous actors, blind followers of foreign slogans, fanatics, communalists, rubberstamps or thumb-impressionists and hired lobbyists. The fair name of democracy should not be tarnished by electing ignoble characters. We have to systematically educate the masses as also the representatives in Yoga.

One striking reason for this malaise, on deep analysis, would appear to be that we tend to put down or degrade talent in the present system apart from the reservations for the backward and other groups on certain considerations which should not exist. The miserable conditions of the poorer people should open our eyes. It is heart-breaking to see young people immolating themselves in protest against the Reservation formula due to misapprehensions. We are not making such reservations in sports and games. Then only the best talent can come up taking the country and the people as a whole forward. Good intentions to achieve an egalitarian society are defeated paradoxically by very means of reservations if it creates vested interests. Facilities, encouragements and all other comforts can be provided with discrimination, but the race should be thrown open to all. Then only the yogic ideal at the macro level can take root for the tree of society to sprout forth towards the supreme goals in all directions. If we prevent talent and merit from public patronage we can only hope for stunted growth and a psychological regression will set in, making the best minds frustrated for not being born into some listed classes of people. A genetic regression blotting out the urge for excellence will set in. It is like a Biological formula for eliminating a species. Though physically born in upper classes, the mental quality would be missing in the beings. The lower classes will aspire to become more backward in the next life. A sort of destructive psychic dementation will be established in all minds or activities and the nation will go down the drain. Why are we still poor among the poorest nations in the world with all our acclaimed resources and natural endowments even after decades of Independence?

In the present times, we find extraordinary talents in men but, they are directionless. That's why from a recent study it was concluded that the chances are dwindling for producing really great persons as in ancient times in any field of creativity. One simple example can be found in the legal field. Though certain individuals have the 'gift of the gab' and achieved enormous monetary success in the profession they cannot be called great because money can purchase them to support any point of view. In other words, whoever can afford them, will get their services. Almost all activities are getting the services of such great talents, but they are devoid of the sense of nobility, justification and purpose, with the result that the negative aspects get accentuated and overwhelm the rest. The so-called intellectuals betray nature's trust and work at cross purposes if they lose sight of the Yogic concept of the union between the mundane and the divine.

A simple study of the working of our Legislatures and Parliament would show that there is a great need to train the legislators in the mechanics of law-making to meet the needs of the people. Very few show real interest in the working. Many do not have the requisite talents or qualifications. In the legal profession we have sharp tongues and minds, but they can be hired for the wrong causes. Money dictates the disposition of the talents and not the sense of righteousness. In the field of Management we equate power with knowledge. Unworthy people are having the upper-hand! Introspection will improve the situation.

The progress of science and technology is stupendous. With Super Computers and Artificial Intelligence, we are almost reaching the limits of comprehension. Expertise is available on tap on unprecedented scale. But then alas! all this can defeat the very purpose if the direction is lost. For example, a brilliant lawyer can be engaged for or against a cause, depending on the price and circumstances. In other areas of human activity also, intelligence is encashed at every opportunity without a real contribution to growth and material productivity. In a sense, this can even be termed as parasitical idleness on a colossal scale when the same energies can be ploughed towards giving more results for the happiness of man and good of society.

There is no dearth of talent in the country. But narrow personal preference and selfish designs can result in Cinderella situations. The silent agony of suppressed talent scorches the land. Let us not contribute to this catastrophe. Swami Vivekanada castigated the educated people who shut their eyes to this responsibility as 'traitors'. Hot-headed monsters, incompetent buffoons, ineffective imbeciles and slick-tongued imposters should give place to well-informed and benevolent gentlemen with sysmpathy and solicitude for all. This is how Gandhiji felt in his last days. The seriousness of the problem warranted the use of such strong language as above. We should not slide back from the progress we have made so far. Should we make our beloved motherland a 'waste land' of bureaucracy with shrubs, thorns, cacti and stones parading as paragons? Late Nobel Laureate Sir C.V. Raman deeply lamented our total apathy and astonishing antagonism towards talent and genius.

Power and money should be freely used to patronise people with promise but not personal stooges.

Trust and Openness Essential for Progress

People should not become apprehensive or fear ridden due to Tax Laws, Police network, Permit, Licence, Quota Systems or any administrative or enforcement machinery in general. Fear should give place to friendliness and trust in all walks of life at all levels. Hostility, Persecution and suspicion were colonial characteristics in police and other enforcement departments earlier. Now they should give place to affection, guidance and trust for the people. Public services generally should demonstrate this attitudinal change as a sign of freedom. Gandhiji's famous dictum "The Customer is the most important visitor on our premises...." should be prominently exhibited everywhere and its spirit should be followed with reference to the common man by all public servants, high or low. It will work wonders within a short a time and a new psycho-social vitality will permeate the society.

Bad cases should not make hard law. By far, goodness is the basic nature of human beings which should be liberally promoted by all systems. The penalty clauses in our laws should be minimised e.g. The Companies Act, 1956 is burdened with too many of them throughout. We could not build up a secondary share market or Over-the counter (OTC) Exchange System to boost up public participation in industry. Investment operations should be taken out of the clutches of the vested interests in Big cities and spread all over the country by opening branches in several centres. Industrial growth is scuttled by cumbersome procedures and lack of adaptation to modern financing techniques, However, steps are being taken by government for easier, smoother and faster industrial growth. The progress we have made is meager as compared to the vast potential. Can't we ever achieve the globalisation as Japanese have done as a miracle? Why not even in a small measure? Faulty appraisals, poor R & D, partial recoveries, unchecked sickness, liberal write-offs and Cinderella situations should be scrupulously avoided. Managers should be surcharged with a sense of National purpose beyond personal preference. It is spiritualisation in a manner speaking. Fortunately, there are still some souls who are amenable to this metamorphosis. A spirit of openness and readiness with a will to achieve results can change the scenario. Several areas in the Commercial and Industrial laws can be simplified by rationalisation and liberalisation. Like in other areas, the lethargy and criminality that are built into the legal systems being appropriate to a slave nation, cannot be got over by mere perfunctory or cosmetic measures, but need a radical reform. This will remain a mirage so long as making money is the main preoccupation of the mentors in every field, as different from the contribution to the quality of life which was the sole theme of the sages of yore.

Openness is another value which has gained great importance in free societies. Secrecy, Confidentiality, Vigilance etc. are identified with administration and vice versa. There is somehow a general feeling of management that softness is a risk and that openness will whittle down authority. The colonial systems worked with a whip in hand, like the mine owners driving the labour to extract more ore. Disbanding these suspicious systems based on mistrust in human goodness is long overdue. It pays in the long run to put faith in dignity and goodness of human life at all levels. By sincere and vigorous efforts this philosophy can permeate an entire organisation. Deliberate miscreants will become practically nil. The suspicion, criminality, penalties etc., built into our systems on an elaborate scale at every turn, speak ill of a civilized and free society. Managements will not regret for putting faith in human nature which is basically good and noble. In earlier times, the unfair and barbarous competition for survival developed obnoxious systems, undermining the dignity and welfare of man. We can now afford to reverse or put an end to these systems to give a new lead and a new management culture.

It may be difficult to strictly categorise all human activities into pigeon-holes as it were. But it is equally difficult to defend the subhuman and slavish or barbarous treatment meted out to women in certain systems. However, many broad universal principles have been drawn from the living experience through centuries of human existence. This is the ethos of civilisation.

Time Consciousness and Time Management

Time consciousness and time management should become the cardinal principles for individuals and institutions. The time wasted in idle pursuits, paperwork, procedures, litigations, mass gatherings, agitations etc. is colossal. The mass media like T.V., Radio, and Films take away precious time and retard creative and intellectual growth. The vulnerable section of the society and children in impressionable age are continuously being exposed to unabashed violence, sex and crime exhibited in films. The ideals set before the people are of very poor quality because most of the actors and artists are not known for their family background or ethical motivation. There are several areas which call for concerted efforts to cut down delays so that time can be saved for improving the quality of life.

Time is eternal. Space is its creation. The entire universe and the phenomenal world emanated from it. Matter exists, changes and dissolves in the scale of time. All the transformation in nature including its animate and inanimate manifestations, is like a play enacted on the stage of time which is the subtle principle that runs through and outlasts all. The greatest of thinkers or philosophers laid down as a rule that we should constantly remind ourselves of the importance of time. This operates as a tonic for the well-being of man in his work for peace and prosperity in worldly pursuits. "Time and Tide wait for none". "A minute lost, is lost forever", "Take time by the forelock". Many such proverbs have gained currency.

One striking fact is that, of all created beings, humans alone seem to have apparent control of time at their disposal. The animals are mainly guided by their instincts and environment. But there is a discernible periodicity or time cycle in the happenings and events in nature. Planetary movements, seasons and similar celestial and terrestrial phenomena have a regularity. Even in the plant world, budding, flowering and fruition occur according to a plan, as it were. There are some plants which come to bloom only once in several years. The variations and differences in the chronology of growth and occurrences are myriad. A little observation and contemplation will make one wonder one at the infinite and inexhaustible variety of ways this time cycle in nature operates. When and how did "movement" originate? It is a big riddle.

Every person should be made to feel the value of time and given proper motivation. This will in turn generate nation building activity in every way out of the free will, cooperation, enthusiasm and aspiration of every person. Flexible work schedules, 4 day work-week for women, job sharing and Temps are some latest methods to reduce boredom and increased productivity, creativity and quality in all routine jobs and other areas as well. Everyone shall feel the joy of fulfillment in the day-to-day events and responsibilities in life by attending to them with utmost care in every detail. This will herald an era of national resurgence, providing validity and meaning to our lives. It may appear to be a huge riddle as to how to find effective employment for all the people as a consequence of eliminating idleness totally. Is it not a fact that the entire population including the idle lot is being fed from some source or other? It is estimated that in India, we still have millions of acres of barren lands which can be brought under cultivation. Likewise, digging of wells and canals, laying of roads and dams, planting of trees and watering them and so many such activities can be promoted to utilise the idle time of the entire population. Not only in the 7 lakhs and odd villages throughout India but also in urban areas and cities, active habits and beneficial progrmmes can be organised as part of the social ethos contributing to the growth of national wealth, involving every individual in the process. It is a stark reality that lakhs of man-hours are wasted in futility and a whole nation known for resourcefulness and potentialities is languishing due to idleness. The supreme need is to build up time consciousness and positive involvement in growth by deliberate and vigorous efforts of management. They should also systematically educate all employees in cleanliness, civic sense, health and human values. This will inject a new psychosocial vitality in the industrial world.

People have to learn how to effectively utilise the time and human resources. Time is like income which we should spend, invest and save to purpose. According to Hindu Chrono-Psychical chart, the twilight hours are known as "Asurasandhya" or the devils' time when the human mind becomes somewhat negative and substandard. Peter Drucker, in his "Managing in Turbulent Times" treats time as one of the resources besides knowledge. Therefore, we have to devote the best time available to our work.

Some Lessons from Nature

Living close to nature and observing it as frequently as possible contributes to the development of personality and promotes character. Children should particularly be given this opportunity in abundant measure. This builds confidence in oneself and quality into the decisions. There is always something great in what is natural and something natural in what is great. We can draw inspiration for techniques like task-definition and solution-development which can be universally applied. It promotes equilibrium or identity between a person and his work. To quote Thomas Carlyle "Blessed is he who has found his work; let him ask for no other blessedness".

India has been discredited as a 'land of delays' in the modern world. The bureaucratic system contributed to this in no small measure. 'Passing the buck' appears to be the perpetual pastime of people in service. Representations, appeals, agitations etc. are galore. This is attributable to the lack of faith in the quality of decisions besides selfishness to outwit the others at any cost. Lack of self-confidence is the main handicap. Closeness to nature in the formative years operates as a tonic against the above deficiencies in human beings.

One may learn a great lot from the lives of Abraham Lincoln and Mahatma Gandhi who can be said to have had their fill from Nature. During the Civil War when a lady tried to comfort

Lincoln with the words "I am sure God is on our side" his repartee "The important thing is whether we are on God's side" is indicative of the natural source of his strength. When Gandhiji was asked why he postponed by three weeks to advise a kid to take less sweets when requested by her mother, his remark "Three weeks ago I was also addicted to sweets" shows the Nature of his character. Several examples of character-building processes involved in Nature's laws can be deduced from the lives of the noble souls who sustained mankind's growth through their words and deeds.

THE AUTHOR

Before the blazing sun of Brahman
I lighted the candle of my life;
And into the deep and deathless ocean
I delivered the drop of my life.

Let others be great and glitter with gold
And rule the kingdoms future or old,
May it be mine the Plight of the lowliest
May I be dead so humble but honest.

– Muchimilli

8

All is One-One is All

All is One–One is All

Truly, Yoga is universal. With the tremendous advancement in space technology and cosmology we now realise that the entire human race on this small globe of ours is but one family as declared in our ancient wisdom "Vasudhaiva Kutumbakam". It is well-nigh impossible for the mind to comprehend the secret or purpose of creation and the ultimate goal of human life (Yato Vacho Vivartante). It may suffer a total internal reflection as opined by the greatest of scientists, Einstein. But the sages insisted on the wisdom when they said "Jnanadevatu Kaivalyam" or "Prajnam Brahma". All religious dogma is tomfoolery and tinsel if enquiry is forbidden. **Intuitive insight revealed to the ancient seers that there is a state of Realisation which is the ultimate Truth.** They designated this as the Supreme or Brahman. (In a way Abraham or Ibraham sounds in rhyme with Brahman). At lesser levels, doubts arise about this very proposition. Therefore, the sages have repeatedly enjoined on themselves that they shall not repudiate the Brahman or vice versa e.g. Sama Veda (Shanthi Path) contains this declaration and undertaking in the words

"Anirakaranamastu". The knower becomes the known. (Brahmavid Brahmaiva Bhavati). It was also realised that to experience this supreme state the human intellect should be fired with imagination, strength and effulgence. The prayers in the earliest of scriptures, Rig Veda, were directed towards this objective e.g. Rig Veda Samhita embodies the famous efficacious Gayatri Mantra pleading for this inspiration and radiance. Similar expressions are also found in almost all the scriptures, religious utterances, songs and pronouncements, in all the world. A sincere and open-minded study would convince us of the basic unity in the apparent diversity of religious ideas and practices. Because of the lack of questioning spirit and genuine enquiry by the so-called educated of the present times, religious bigotry and fanaticism are increasing and the priest class by what-ever name called, are 'ruling the roost".

The highest good and joy of life consists in working with a passion for human improvement. This is the exalted end of all human endeavour, contemplation, reason, learning and spirituality. This selfless attitude towards life and creation is stimulationg and exhilarating. It brings about qualitative transformation and makes the humblest of lives most sublime. They are truly the salt of the earth who cherish this goal of life by working ceaselessly, indifferent to fame and preferring anonymity. The golden strands of their work and thoughts bind earth with the heavens. They are the source and inspiration for the vibrations of love permeating and sustaining the entire universe and especially the human race. Let us learn to respect and follow them.

It is not difficult to realise the objective if we carefully follow the message in the following memorable lines by Muchimilli:

The Universe is yours
If you love all mankind as your own.
This Oneness and Manyness
Is called Brahman or OM
The lord, Supreme, Almighty or Unknown:

His children, messengers, messiahs or men
proclaim the same truth about Him
And preach Love, kindness and help
Irrespective of colour, creed, or the rest.
So, reflect on your Godliness
And work for lasting peace and happiness,
Be a grain of the soil and enrich it,
Be like a fountain, a shower of grace,
A flower for worship, a fruit of health,
Giving away all the time and receiving more blessings
Working with joy and improving the surroundings,
Treating all as your own and making them one
With faith in future and human endeavour
Shedding the superstitions and fears of ignorance,
Predictions of idlers and debilitating horoscopes,
Rising above pettiness faithlessness and penury,
Be yourself, bold, not as a fanatical blot on humanity
But as the beneficiary of the best of Mankind's glory.
Be a True Man, unbiased, unruffled and exemplary,
Magnanimous, Action-oriented and Non-violent.

Largely, human life is transmutable. Significantly, there are hardly four blood groups for the entire human race as compared to the myriad classifications we have made of people. In truth, even this variation loses meaning when we realise that our origin and destiny are one the same. Selfishness as distinguished from enlightened self-interest, destroys the entire edifice of human progress at micro and macro levels. One should try to merge into eternity like a waft of fresh air which is possible only through love of humanity and service beyond self. This determines the quality of life.

The great law giver 'Manu' propounded that substance outweighs all Forms and the pursuit of righteousness and peace supercedes all distinctions and division-"Dharme Nasramo Karanam". This is the spirit of Christ when he said-"The pure in heart shall see God". One can quote Veda, Gita, Guru Granth,

Koran, Bible and so many other scriptutes and sayings to substantiate the above principle. But suffice it to say that the sun is only one for us and how foolish it is to look for a darker side with our predilections or take the images as real. Let us imagine, if not treat, the whole world as our home and all its people as one great family "Vasudhaiva Kutumbakam". This is the minimum mental preparation for a good human being.

A child will pick up the language of the people who bring it up. There is no inherited language formula of genetic significance in the child. This is a revealing situation. Likewise, human beings have different blood groups which are not restricted or dependent on their language, place of birth, country, colour and other such divisions. But, unfortunately, the people of the world are divided by the most narrow and irrelevant geographical and physical considerations on an almost permanent basis with the result that the differences are perpetuated and enmity is created. The barbaric groups in ancient and medieval times could not think on universal level and believed in feudalistic or slavish systems. Their mentors were also like uncultured thugs or plunderes who believed in killing human beings. Yogic thought will make us realise that the entire mankind is one huge family and the differences based on which we fight amongst ourselves are not worthy of modern civilization and the progress we have made over the centuries.

The spirit of tolerance is the test of true religion. The surest way to work towards harmony and simplicity is to remember that death will remove everyone from the scene including our little ego. Having been born as human beings, let us lead ourselves as beautiful and worthy children of God and make the world a better and happier place to live in. Even the tiniest contribution in this regard gets registered in the time scale of Eternity. Otherwise our life becomes a wasteful burden for Mother Earth. The several forms and names attributed to the Almighty through the ages are different means to comprehend and experience the glory of the Supreme in its myriad facets. With this understanding, we will do well to relise the truth in the saying "God's one; Worship Him Universally". This provides validity and meaning to human life. This should be the path to world peace.

Flowery speeches unless followed by the fruit of action are futile. We liberally use the words, "We are like a family", when referring to organizations, societies etc. and also the world. Mostly it is a mere lip–service by self-centered people, insincere to the concept. All the misery in the world will simply vanish if this conviction of being one family is truly realised in practice. This requires enormous effort by the educated people of the world to change their motives and serve the cause of human progress at all levels. When we speak more, the likelihood of speaking lies is also more. This applies mutatis mutandis to acquisition of wealth also. When more and more personal wealth is amassed the chances are that it is mostly tainted. Virtue lies in moderation.

There are many unique features of India viz. the Himalayas, the rivers, the purity of the waters, the range of flora, fauna, climate etc. compared to other countries. Many eminent intellectuals of all lands have paid glorious tributes to the spiritual genius, profound philosophy, literary grandeur and cultural ethos which from part of our heritage. One marvels at their undisputed testimony. A hundred great names can be mentioned. The sun truly rose in the East and spread its rays far and wide. The Supreme, true to its nature, is conceived as one but the paths are many. All are children of God. His love is unbounded. There is no room for enmity, war, hatred, fanaticism or other evils. In modern world we should realise that there is only one human culture. After Independence, we are a free nation and are like a family. This is our dear Mother land and we are all her beloved children.

A house divided by suspicion is hell. Heaven is where the differences are resolved and mutual trust and affection are in evidence. There is no need for any community or religious group to always look peculiar or different from others in such a house.

People should be persuaded not to exhibit their opulence, poverty or any other eccentricities. It is also not good to exhibit religious symbols and fanatical traits in one's dress and manners.

The so-called diversity should be based on individual freedom and not on bigotry and compulsion. Further, why carry weapons amidst fellow countrymen unless one is always afraid of or planning an attack? This is contrary to the profession of brotherhood, trust, courtesy, love and goodwill. It creates suspicion and fear. Weapons poison freedom.

The Language Barrier-the Hindrance to Progress

We make such a fetish of the numerous regional and national languages that they have become strong disintegrating forces. Certain languages have developed International character and strength which should be accepted magnanimously with grace to subserve the common interest of global communication and integration. Taking an exaggerated example, just as precious metals, jewels or beads need not vie for commonality with iron, brass etc. the local languages or dialects need not be stretched too far. Everything has its place. A university is not a museum. What is the dishonour in accepting universal language standards when similar advancement is adopted in other fields like Medicine, Engineering, Science and Technology? Do we depend on local quacks for treatment? Don't we find even staunch Gandhians making foreign trips for treatment? Why use the masks in the face of reality?

The quarrels over the different languages in India and abroad make much sorrowful reading. This is the result of giving more importance to mere form rather than the substance. A Yogi would have the discernment to overcome these barriers and exhibits no attachment to the language as such. Imperfect and incomplete languages have cropped up all over the globe like shrubs and mushrooms which the narrow minds try to project as giant trees. Scientific approach will show us that most of these languages are incapable of growing and fulfilling the purposes because of their intrinsic defects in structure, syntax, etymology etc.

Vis-à-vis English, many of the Indian languages are undeveloped, imperfect, incomplete and phonetically deficient. Sanskrit is truly the mother of languages and is technically rich in etymology and world building methods. Luckily, Hindi has inherited some richness including the script. Unimaginative and parochial minds are trumpeting the greatness of these imperfect languages beyond all proportion resulting in a psychological estrangement and antagonism in our polity. This is also a disintegrating factor. English has a great role to play in future also.

The western countries progressed enormously before our own eyes. Their modern outlook on religion and language was largely responsible for it. Our hypocrisy, fanaticism and false pride in primitive habits are ruining us.

Amelioration of Human Suffering Trough Psycho-social Vitality

Can we eradicate from the face of the earth, suffering, diseases, accidents, poverty and such other painful situations? To the extent they are man-made, the answer is 'yes', though it is easier said than done. With the nuclear arsenal it is easier to destroy the Earth itself or the entire mankind. Natural calamities and many disasters may seem to be beyond human control. But, we can certainly mitigate the effects by planned action. There are some preventive measures also. It calls for cohesion and rallying of all world resources, just as in a human body any suffering is shared in totality. This can be projected on a global scale to build up the necessary psycho-social vitality for ameliorating suffering universally. Muchimilli brings out the spirit in the following poem:

Peace and plenty?
Was it ever there?
It never was
And never will be
Except in man's
Goodness and care,
For,
If men do spare
Their surplus fare
There sure is
Peace and plenty.

Perversions and eccentricities have to be curbed for enabling healthier and happier pursuits in life in the larger interests of the society. Adulteration of foodstuffs, spurious goods, pollution of every kind, obscene advertisements and films, smoking in public, including such scenes in T.V serials as indirect advertisements, destruction of public property, increasing litigation and wasteful expenditure are some of the avoidable evils.

The parochial systems and pampering of certain classes or groups may also ruin the country's progress if they create vested interests against talents and merits which are vital for growth. There is a Vedic saying that if a cow weeps, the land will be scorched. Why create huge land reserves for tigers, panthers etc. and starve the innocent cows? Evil is growing because of misplaced sympathies. Merit is not to be crushed and condemned by mediocrity. This may be the real corruption plaguing the country. If any progress is possible, it is only because there are still people who respect learning and who seek the truth against odds. The Freedom and sincerety of their minds is the guarantee for growth in all walks of life.

Prayer-the Medicine for Purification of Mind

Just as the heart purifies the bloodstream, so also is prayer with reference to the thought process. This influences directly or indirectly the action. Prayer inspires, ennobles, enriches and expands the consciousness. The action of a catalyst, according to science, is mysterious. Likewise, prayer fructifies action. As the language of the heart, it is pure. Forms, images, words, manners and other multifarious paraphernalia associated with worship are secondary. They should not defeat the purpose of peace and happiness. Even the greatest rationalist, Voltaire, after deep deliberation, concluded that even if there is no God, there is need to invent one. This fills the void or gaps in human psyche and brings about orderliness, cleanliness, discipline, hopefulness, philanthrophy, penitence, thankfulness etc. within and without. It helps towards the pursuit of excellence; it flows naturally like the rivers moving towards the ocean or the iron filings being drawn towards the magnet. There is some strange fulfilment, equilibrium, peace and ultimately happiness in the act of prayer. It can be said, "If you fear God, you need not fear man." Differently expressed, it comes to the same thing as saying, if you love God, you tend to love yourself and the whole creation, for, thereby you transcend the limitations of the embodied. No qualifications or detailed exercises or initiation is required. Even absolute silence is a form of prayer. Better be silent and allow the Lord to speak. This kindles the innermost core of the being which is happiness itself. A ripend soul is full of prayer. It is attained after many births as declared in Gita *"Bahunam Janmanam unte"*.

Universality and freedom characterise a true prayer. No shackles; no regimentation. It is like the lotus of the heart coming to full bloom to receive the rays of the sun. It includes both the personal and impersonal aspects. People set ideals before them and deified them. They drew inspiration and comfort from the strength and disposition of the Supreme to give them succour. A weakling who cannot protect himself or a fugitive who could not face a battle cannot offer protection to others. The spirit of sacrifice for the wellbeing of others and compassion for the poor was the real bedrock of true religion. A spirit of communion or harmony with nature also gave rise to different symbols of worship. Forms, though helpful, are not essential; they only provide endearment and perception. There is a beautiful and innocent child in every person throughout life, like the tender twig on every tree, which finds the thrill of joy in the world of fantasy. We should not harden sensibilities and cripple the feeling for creativity. The mind, with about 15,000 million nerve cells has to be vibrant. Intuitive perception and psychic experimentation revealed that certain forms and symbols developed from nature and human ingenuity, satisfy its genius and provide tranquillity, peace and joy. Some cells of the mind account for the feelings of kindness, tolerance, human consideration etc. as instilled by enlightened religious attitudes. Devoid of the magnanimity and multi-dimensional exposure, the mental cells stagnate, degenerate and develop destructive propensities.

Just as beauty, strength and other ennobling and acclaimed qualities are seen and experienced through different forms, the Divine or the Supreme is represented by certain enchanting, mythical, captivating and colourful forms. Alongside, there are also symbols like Ravan, Cross, etc. which bring to mind the most heinous, inhuman and despicable events and characters which should be shunned. The Divine is mostly depicted with a beautiful charming and awe-inspiring face and other physical attributes. Facelessness is not favoured. However, superstitions, sentiments, emotions and bigotry or fanaticism will not make one enlightened. Thus, the theories of non-dualism or Monism aimed at universal appeal have been developed. The logical extreme would lead to the postulation of the Supreme as being Omnipotent, Omniscient and Omnipresent. It transforms the man, dissolving his little ego, while trying to find the true identity in relation to the ideal. As the poet expressed it "He prayeth best who loveth best both things great and small". Ill-will and the inclination to harm have no place in the heart of a man of prayer. His simple motto in life would be "Be good, Do Good". This sublimates the emotions and radiates warmth, a sure sign of happiness.

A beautiful and simple though indirect way to instil a sense of belonging to the country and pride in the culture, which in turn imparts a consciousness for utilising the time constructively for self-development and national prosperity, is to make a meaningful prayer a prelude to all activities and compulsory in educational institutions. For this purpose, the prayer should have a theme and motivation and not merely be a description of the glory or a list of names with some emotion. Simply chanting that our country is full of sweet-watered rivers has not provided drinking water even to a city like Chennai. One such prayer which may serve the purpose is given below.

May I be worthy of this land of mine
And lay down my life for its prosperity and gain
May its honour be held so high
And in eternal grandeur its flag shall fly.

May I be strengthened in my resolve to lead
A truthful life in thought, world and deed

And a purposeful life of sacrifice and service
To the poor and needy in their hours of crisis.

May I be helpful in building up the Nation
Into an upright and hardworking Civilisation,
Wasting no time in idle pleasures or ostentation
Till every Indian is free from fear of starvation.

May I truly feel the oneness with all human beings
And never cause them harm by my words or actions
May I strive to promote the spirit of goodwill and tolerance
Which is the human way to individual and world peace.

EPITAPH

Here lies the man who was little known
Except to the few who were all his own
He was a pilgrim to heights divine
And struggled to stem our steep decline
Seeing much hope and some better turn
He left our hearts after a happy sojourn.

– *Muchimilli*

THE DIVINE

With the blessing of birth and follies of youth
I never thought of Thee even in contempt;
But when I stopped my song and stilled my voice
Thou wert there with your loving embrace.

The winds are odd and the tides are swift
Tossing my ship to its core;
But I abandon the rudder and sail adrift
For Thou to steer me clear ashore.

Drowning in the ocean of birth and death
My poor heart sought support in every straw;
But Though wert there readily in a boat
To save me only when I gave up all hope.

You came like a king in elegant array
In a glorious suite, glamorous and gay;

Shrinking in my rags I sneaked on the way
To steal a glimpse and glitter in a ray.

Steadily through the throngs of devotees
I crept close to your feet;
But struck by you splendour, my eyes full of fears
I lost sight of Thee.

Like a poor man who found a treasure
And like a child who claimed a toy,
I revelled in you patronage;
But anxious to aver to the world at large
I become dumb like the bird in a cage.

When the mind is serene and the heart is pure,
With the thoughts of the world all obscure,
The desire for you from deep within
Reveals to me my nature divine.

– *Muchimlli*

9

Play Your Role

Revamping of the Education System

We have corrupted our basic values and thinking by lack of proper direction in our educational system. To give an example, little place is given for Ramakrishna, Vivekananda and Tagore in school books in their home State. Similar is the position of Sankara, Vallathol and Bhattitiri in Kerala. Other States have their own Pseudo-secular Syndromes. This is true in almost all walks of life where self-interest is causing the perversion from the real values. An interesting instance which may look far-fetched is found in people chanting the Hare Rama Mantra with Krishna first. It is like running car in reverse gear i.e. putting Krishna before Rama. The efficacy would be lost in the process. One is at a loss to know why people shout "Bande Mataram" (bind the Mother) instead of Vandemataram when the meanings of the words are diametrically opposite. Vested interests are undermining the very foundation of our society and Dharma is twisted to suit the selfish needs at all levels.

To give another example, the Father of the Nation, Gandhiji, prescribed austerity for the leaders. He desired that the luxurious palaces and colonial buildings should be used in the service of the people. But it is Tweedledum Tweedledee.

It saddens the heart to find that the same colonial pampered living is indulged in with a vengeance. I find great significance in his final word to mankind viz. "Hey Ram" thus invoking the spirit of Rama in the last breath of his life.

Children have pure hearts and open minds. They do not see things with any bias based on caste, creed, religion, region etc. It is unfortunate that they are being subjected to discrimination on these grounds during their formative years in matters of admission to schools, professional courses and later on in getting jobs etc. This poisons the thinking and gives a feeling that they are being let down by the nation despite their best efforts. Those who lost hopes committed self-immolation in a ghastly way in recent years. The scenes of self-immolation by innocent meritorious students, printed strikingly in magazines and newspapers, should open our eyes to the crime of discrimination on considerations of caste, class, language etc. In olden days, everyone aspired to evolve into higher states of existence and knowledge. Now the advantages of being backward are made so attractive that the desire for excellence and higher knowledge is scorched. This is a crime against humanity. "Backwardness" is filling the minds of people. The country has to pay a high price for it because undeserving, ill-qualified and incompetent people are patronised in perference to the meritorious and talented persons. Class hatred is implanted everywhere. Education should provide proper motivation and should not create bad-blood, dejection and hatred on the basis of caste, class, language etc. Adopting the economic criteria, we may provide free tuition, books and other amenities to the students besides other subsidies and monetary benefits to the poor families. The important thing is that the competitive spirit should not be erased from their minds. Hinduism highlights human spirit without castes and classes and aims at world citizenship of man.

My hear is bleeding for the children of this country,
For, most schools, if not all, stink with poverty and misery
The missionary and public schools curiously care for the rich pedigree,
About the lot of the remaining schools, the less said the better,
you'll agree;

Abject surrender, helplessness and apathy are the parents' lot
The nation is sacrificing its children at an irredeemable cost,
They live like worms in dark holes, dust spots and what not,
They are utterly neglected when their hearts are tender and soft,

Why are the schools like this even after decades of Independence?
Can we not have a good building in every locality for instance
With some ventilation, light, seats, etc. and cleanliness
And a few well-paid teachers with a loving look on their faces!

All our lives, efforts and trumpet-blowings
Become futile and worthless as rats' borrowings
All our taxes, profits and public spendings
Become unreal as mad men's rejoicings
If we do not care for our children at least now
And build schools of health, happiness and love.

Let every child feel he is take care of by the county
And he will grow into a patriot and work for its prosperity.
This is what Gandhiji bemoaned bitterly in utter desperation
That our education is devoid of National Orientation.
For, a degenerate nation neglects its own children
And subjects them to cultural and character ruination.

You may have no children or they may have all comforts at their command,
But don't forget that you have a duty towards your poor Motherland,
And you can't be happy when she is shedding sorrowful tears
For the care and schooling of her innocent "Little Dears'.

– *Muchimilli*

The Need for Useful Publications

Words seem to influence people more than thoughts and actions. We wonder to know what were the first words spoken. It is said that they were heard from some divine source which cannot be questioned. Now, we have hundreds of languages in the world. Some of them are very advanced with technical and scientific vocabulary. According to linguistics, the Sanskrit language has the richness in etymology, word-structure and felicity of phrase like gold amongst the metals. There are many world languages which have acquired the quality and resourcefulness for every shade and nuance of expression. We see that most literature of historical nature was concerned with Royal intrigues or other archaic themes which are totally irrelevant to us at the present juncture of evolution. Still, crores of rupees are spent in publishing such volumes in all languages. Writers, and institutions should have a policy to bring out only the minimum of such literature. We should concentrate on research and scientific works. The rest is all gibberish, degrading and wasteful. Some words are imbued with potency. Utterance of them will set in wholesome vibrations. Noble thoughts associated with them may also generate healthy emotions in people. It is now established medically and scientifically that they bring about chemical changes in the body's metabolism. This may be the reason for the influence of epic poetry of the saints of yore.

There is a universal saying that the voice of people (vox populi) is the voice of God. Similarly, the utterances of sages (Rishi-Vakyam) have also the divine stamp. Poetry is also believed to spring from the spark of creativity and the Supreme is described in the Veda as the poet of poets (Kavih Kaveenam). By these standards, most publications consuming countless tons of paper which is produced by destroying the entire forest wealth, are colossal waste of efforts. Mostly, parochial and mediocre minds are projected as venerable leaders and their memory is sought to be perpetuated even overlooking giant historic personalities. For example, it makes one sad to see the plethora of memorials and publications honouring all and sundry by their self-seeking supporters, neglecting the great teachings and ideals of the Father of the Nation, Mahatma Gandhi, who would have been submerged in the quagmire of petty politics but for the redeeming efforts of a few thoughtful persons including the film maker, Richard Attenborouh. Most Ashrams, Societies, Clubs etc., in modern times had escapist origins, some with Anglicised Founders who revelled in fantasy and grandiloquence more than service to National Causes like removing poverty, disease, illiteracy etc. The successors managed to cover up the shallowness and irrelevance of these memorials by manipulation and commercialisation with a dog-in-the-manger tenacity. Their publications and other activities are redundant and superficial, representing stagnation without real growth for public benefit. They are a refuge to idlers and lotus-eaters. We should open up self-centred institutions to public gaze and use, removing the cult or denominational abuse.

Women's Role in the Society

Nature also, to a large extent, dictates or lays down one's place in the scheme of things. We should promote harmony by accepting this dispensation or arrangement. To give an example, Mother Teresa has concluded after decades of public life and noble service as a nun, "A woman cannot have a better place than the house. The greatest gift is to be a mother and dutiful wife."

In the poorer sections of society, all the members do manual work to make both ends meet. Life is a mere sand-clock for them! But educated women are misguided by the slogan of equality with men to the detriment of Home Management by clamouring for routine office jobs which can be offered to more needy persons. Their creative genius and aesthetic endowments are criminally wasted. They are employed generally for their glamour and not for their suitability or qualities. Films are ruining the image of Indian womanhood where the same persons act as wife and husband, sister and brother, mother and son etc. Women excel in Nursing, teaching, fine Arts and other professions which come naturally to them. Equality with men has no meaning. The Head of the Scotland Yard, while visiting India remarked that the crime rate is lowest in India due to strong 'family bonds' and women's role is vital therein. It may be difficult to strictly categorise all human activities into pigeon-holes as it were. But it is equally difficult to defend the subhuman and slavish or barbarous treatment meted out to women in certain systems. However, many broad universal principles have been drawn from the living experience through centuries of human existence. This is the ethos of civilisation.

The Role of Educated Persons

Intuitive wisdom is of the same nature. The same gold is exhibited as different ornaments; the same electricity lights up different apartments. All over the world, wherever nature provided the facilities for growth and the Elements were conducive for settlement, human beings lived in groups and organised themselves. After the intuition and wisdom of the founders faded away the followers mistook the external practices as the real essence and tried to adhere to them even when they migrated. This resulted in incongruity and conflict. The rigidity and lack of adaptation to local systems passed off as religious fervor. At this point of time, after centuries of growth, with the historical material available for scrutiny, intelligence built up in evolution, universal vision becoming almost a reality, it should be possible for man to discern the common nexus in creation and the purposefulness of knowledge. Narrow, domestic and fanatical attitudes can easily be dissolved in the larger interests of happiness and progress of mankind. The responsibility has to be taken by the educated members of the society to analyse the causes of differences and integrate the underlying currents into a unified field of modern and civilized religion. Otherwise, the fanatics will forever hold the country to ransom.

Even if it is taken as an inexorable and absolute theory, survival of the fittest is not a barbarous principle of negation of life. Man is more than a mere sum-total of genes and his body is not a mere adaptation. The old theories of Darwin and Sigmund Freud or the modern 'B.Mod' of Prof. B.F. Skinner should not mislead us. After the long process of evolution we have arrived at the final stage and we can now herald an era of fruition. Muchimilli brings out the message in the following query:

The cow feeds on grass and gives its nourishing milk;
The mango labours on the rocks and delivers us the fruit;
The bee wanders to many a flower and gathers us the honey;
But what have we done in our turn as the donee?

His dream of the world as flowing with honey and milk can be realised if the educated people of the world pay heed to certain basic values of life. In the manner of Christ, Mohamad, Buddha, Mahavira and others, it had fallen to Mahatma Gandhi to practise the noble principles of truth and non-violence and give the lead as a 'kindly light' amidst darkness and gloom. Such examples are found in history and we do well to remember their contribution to human progress. Every human being is potentially divine in that he can contribute to the quality of life by self-analysis and application. No darkness is too great to overcome for even a small candle. This is not idealism but a practical example within the reach of every person.

Every educated person should share the sadness or responsibility for allowing evils, superstitions etc. to grow without so much as even a mental repudiation or silent conviction. It is not to be left only to the politicians or Government to curb them. The effect of collective will is like the voice of God. Even if this thought is spread and taken to the people, it can transform entire societies and a new universal civilization can be heralded. Mass communication technology is so advanced that a good thought can be implanted in the hearts of people the world over in a short time.

Creeds, cults, denominations and other barriers have multiplied. Divisions are created amongst people on considerations of caste, State, region, nationality, colour etc. Examples can be given of such pettiness and selfishness riding roughshod over goodness and truth in all the different parts of the world. This is a fact of life everywhere. But the capacity of the common people to bear the sufferings and oppression of these elements is mystifying. True democracy remains an ideal and many societies are denied even the rudimentary characteristics of freedom. This casts an immense responsibility on the educated people of the world to open their minds to the real situation and come out boldly to assert the universal values of love, brotherhood and peace. This is the true purpose of life at the macro level. This can be brought about by the individuals themselves becoming conscious of this phenomenon. Similar thoughts in people, even if they are silent, will generate a global will and materialise a state of existence in tune with the thoughts.

The Media to Propagate the Message

The real problem is how to bring the wisdom into the labyrinth of modern systems. Fortunately, the stupendous advancement in communication technology of radio, T.V., etc., can carry the message to the people all over the world almost instantaneously. This should be harnessed constructively and productively. Very potent, positive, life-giving, healthy, happy and fruitful thoughts can be spread and implanted in people's minds. The whole world can be transformed within a short time into a heavenly body of peace-loving, prosperous and harmonious human family. Respect for learning and dedication to duty are the two essential prerequisities for progress. They are like the two eyes. A person imbued with them will find fulfillment and joy in day-to day events and responsibilities in life by attending to them with utmost care in every detail. This will eliminate the parasites, idlers in the form of astrologers, fanatics, politicians, preachers, priests etc. A vigorous, creative, buoyant, dynamic and progressive society will emerge which will overcome all barriers of caste, creed, colour, nationality, religion etc.

Distribution of wealth should not result in poverty for all in due course. Futher, idleness is another great impediment to progress. Most people indulge in unproductive engagements wasting their talents and resources. Productive orientation is woefully lacking in our programmes and systems. History and luxury getting more importance in private as well as public lives. Pleasing the 'little ego' has become the pre-occupation for powers that be everywhere. Volumes are printed consuming tones of paper dealing with private lives and details of no consequence. Powerful public media like, TV and Radio project the passing personalities more than providing constructive programmes for nation-building. A modicum of entertainment is always prescribed as desirable.

But a mountain of farce with only a pinch of purposefulness cannot serve the nation at the present juncture. Cacti and pebbles should not be paraded as Paragons in public view. Valuable time is wasted in pettiness and sycophancy. Besides, we have to build up a whole new generation of people who can face the challenges of the modern world and build a prosperous society for the entire country. Thus, the programmes should have orientation, educating the people in all requirements for a purposeful and happy living in the modern world. So much work remains to be done for providing even basic amenities to millions of people. True spiritual approach lies in spirited activities for construction of schools, training institutes, laying of roads, dams, and other irrigation facilities besides housing and health-care all over the country. Enormous time is wasted for politiking and gathering people for self-same superfluous speeches of all and sundry, every now and then. The powerful medium of T.V. can now change the habits of people and direct them towards more meaningful lives of action and nobility as a solution to this malady. The T.V. Programmes should *engender* self-development and good citizenship. Further, culture is confused with Archaelogy and is presented mostly as Tribalism with grotesque scenes etc. Fashion is shown as vulgarity and the youngsters learn what and where to look for! Respect for womanhood is being undermined by the cine images and indecent postures presented on T.V. An instinct for obscenity is being planted and nurtured by our cultural demigods. Some evil may be part of life but it cannot be made a way of life. We have to inculcate restraint and refined sentiments in people by deliberate and drastic reorientation of our programmes. (This is different from the Slave Morality of 'Nietzsche'.) With the right inspiration reaching every home and heart and with real concern for technical advancement and cultural excellence, a new India shall be born to fulfill our dreams of the 21st Century.

THE SUPREME

Coeval with stars my spirit with them doth last
Till all the worlds and future recede into the past;

I am the beginning and end of all things that are cast
With names and forms but they return to me, at last.

A speck of the sun makes for the totality
Of earth's energy and all its vitality;
I shall spring a thousand suns into sight
And shut them if I so choose in the palm of my might.

I scan the stars and fix them in their place
I command the sun and the moon to run round their race;
When awake I manifest my many-splendoured grace
When in slumber I take in the whole universe.

My dreams are reality in the worlds
My manifestation knows no bounds;
Eternity is my hand-maid ever
Creation and dissolution are all my power.

When virtue and truth have lost their pride,
When vice and wiles will whelm and boom.
I trample the worlds in my angry stride
And doom the stars to gloom.

My breath is the music of the universe
And the wind is its wave:
I shall lull the worlds asleep
When to my abode I leave.

– *Muchimilli*

10

Awake, Arise and Regenerate

Evolutionary Process of Changing the Indian Social Fabric to Regenerate and Methods for the Same

In the good old days, when Nature was bountiful with few mouths to feed, people devised festivals, rituals, ceremonies, rites etc., with considerable frequency and prolonged fanfare. Personal events like birthday, marriage, obsequies and community celebrations like melas, pilgrimages, pujas, etc. extended over several days to fill the large idle time. The upper classes like priests, rulers and others had, to some extent, exploited the gullibility, ignorance and innocent devotion of the people. Many superstitions and idle theories like astrological predictions, omens and other taboos took root in the idle minds. This affected the spirit of experimentation and scientific innovation e.g. if touching a corpse is taboo, how can surgery be developed! Material comforts declined as activities like building of houses, roads, canals, irrigation facilities, schools etc. were neglected. Mere literary activity, philosophical discourses and building of enormous temples, mosques, churches etc. received more attention with the subjugation of the people by the more powerful rulers. Different religious ideas have also taken roots and created divergent attitudes and differences amongst the people.

This has also weakened the social fabric. Fanaticism grew as there was no adaptation to local conditions and changed needs. Population continued to grow by leaps and bounds, depleting the distributable earnings and food produced in the country. It was expected that the political independence would herald economic independence also. The British devised several systems and laws which were necessary to maintain their hegemony and control over a hostile nation. The bureaucratic set up was stringently attuned to the requirements of the ruling regime. This is largely unsuitable to an independent democratic republic as the psychological orientation should be radically different. People should partake in the development process and feel the joy of freedom to build a destiny for the generations to come.

Many savants have proclaimed India to be the land of spiritual destiny for mankind. Mahatma Gandhi, Vivekananda, Max Mueller, Voltaire, Will Durant and a host of historic personalities accepted that the hope for mankind lies in our culture like the light of the sun being heralded in the dawn from the East. Without bragging about our ancient greatness which attracted explorers from all over the globe to our land, we have to seriously analyse and come to grips with the present-day situation. Almost all right-thinking persons, living saints and even common people feel disheartened at the utter disharmony, violence, hatred, crime, corruption and other evils plaguing our society. The simple principles on which the foundation was laid for a glorious civilization and its growth are now losing their hold and do not carry conviction with the powers that be. 'Respect for learning and Dedication to duty' are the two eyes for the body politic. All material power should be subordinated and made to subserve the above two values of life. This was the very soul or conscience of our ethos as a society. It is also known that power and wealth in whatever manner acquired, would put scales and obstruct proper vision. Confidential Reports and other obnoxious methods helped to kill talent. Likewise, wealth is working against human values.

This is the real cancer of corruption in our society and not the petty foibles of some poor folk. The nation will have to pay the penalty for lack of proper perspectives in the top people even after the avowed strengthening of the grass roots, as wisdom lies in heeding the warnings of the wise and not despising them as prophets of doom or hunting them out from seats of power. Late Noble Laureate Sir C.V. Raman lamented about our total apathy and astonishing antagonism towards talent and genius. Incompetent schemers are catapulted into power. As per the latest World Bank Report, 40% of our population is below poverty line. What are we making of our enormous natural resources? Democracy is not a fool's paradise. We should wake up to the demands of our Constitution and restructure the systems.

Refinement in any field of human activity brings about happiness and peace. To this end, we have to re-evaluate and re-structure our purposes and methods of working. Taking the legal field, as an example, the laws, rules and procedures, instead of serving as levers, are proving to be stumbling blocks and whatever ingenuity or intelligence is found in the legal profession is utilized for making material gains at every opportunity without regard to the ultimate objective of justice. It may sound a harsh judgement, but the fact remains that the price or the fee paid determines the talent that can be hired for a cause. Complicated and bad drafting of laws has added to the multiplicity of litigation. Year after year the backlog of cases is assuming bewildering proportions while the best legal talents are engaged in jugglery of words and legal quibbling. It requires great refinement to bring about the change in the whole atmosphere of enactment of laws, their administration through the official machinery and adjudication of cases in courts, touching the lives of millions of our poor people. The conscience of legal experts should be aroused towards this end.

Similarly, in the field of medicine also we have to make efforts on a war-footing to being down the disease-level. Three-fourths of our population may not pass a reasonably good medical test. There may be a plethora of causes for this malaise. Adulteration of food stuffs, spurious drugs, unhealthy habits, lack of opportunities for physical exercise, commercial attitude in the profession as contrasted with the humanitarian requirements, lack of facilities, are some of the causes which are not difficult to overcome. We have dealt with some problems in the legal profession which is described as "noble and learned" and the medical profession which is "humanitarian in essence". The scenario is the same if not worse, in others also. A spiritual awakening to serve the society to the best of our abilities is wanting. Gandhiji referred to "Talented Thieves" and "Gentleman Rascals" and Vivekananda called them "Traitors".

Strikes, lock-outs and lack of productivity are the factors which plague the industrial scene. Destruction of Public property at the slightest provocation is also causing huge national loss. It is not difficult to mitigate the situation by creating the right attitudes in management and public relations. This calls for intensive drive to instill the feeling of commitment towards national objectives. Feudalistic and sadistic systems and elements have to be curbed. A feeling of participation in the achievement of national progress should be within the reach of all people. This is possible if only we restructure and refine our political, economic and social systems.

The sophistication and progress in human life has been generated or achieved by assiduous application of the intelligence by select brand of people dedicated to their jobs in a spirit of a yogic yearning for truth. Human Resources Development is now needed when all human relations are commercialized for their utilitarian value. However, without a mental commitment for supporting or doing good work, it is seldom possible to make progress. The patronage and avid media coverage given to the barbarous fighting in Boxing and Karate proves that education has not refined our idea of sporting talent. Man's unkindness to man is glorified and gloated over even to this day in several areas which any be metaphorised as Boxing Rings. Education should give us the Courage to disown all diabolical designs to inflict harm on human life except as punishment for proven and unrepentent criminals. Butchery of talent should cease to be the pastime of people with power. Life presents umpteen opportunities to do some good turn or other throughout but we let go the same and indulge in negative action, diminishing the virtue and dignity of human birth. India can be transformed into a great nation if this is sufficiently realised and our energies are applied in harmony with the Gandhian ideal of helping the righteous and the poor objectively.

Gandhiji showed us the way, but we are lured into an existence where wealth accumulates and men decay. All hope is not lost if we realise the folly and follow the right path again. Respect for learning and dedication to duty are the two lines demarcating this path. The lines are faint now, but not totally obliterated. Though liberal and progressive, Gandhiji deprecated the use of foreign goods, drinks, meat etc. , not as his narrow fads, but, inter alia, to save the elite from the lures and fortify the freedom struggle. He stood like a rock for human values. Gandhiji and Vivekananda were the prime heroes who fully marshalled the good old English saying, "That nation would be happy whose honest men could speak as loud as the scoundrels". Their thoughts should be broadcast regularly.

In the ultimate analysis, it is necessary to create an awareness in all the people of the existence of an all-pervasive law above human power, rendering divine dispensation for wrongs done, seen or unseen, irrespective of material success or immediate tangible gains. This notion of punishment for wrongs, provided the motivation for people to avoid unscrupulous or unethical ways of making money and seeking satisfaction of desires. This promotes real purity and not mere show of purity. Thus, the spiritual solution for the present ills of every nature lies in relentlessly canvassing for the above awareness in one and all which was the common feature of life in olden days, but which has been eroded in modern times. On the positive side, one can also experience the joy, in living as a good human being, by practicing even a minimum of the spiritual values outlined above, though initially they may appear to be inconvenient and unnecessary for material success.

Historically, as the State grew in power the Army and the Bureaucracy became strong adjuncts. The Establishment became synonymous with conservative and traditional forces. The liberals or the populist leaders are distinguishable in the struggle for dominance. In the U.S.A. the old war heroes like Washington can be contrasted with popular figures like Reagan and others. In India, heredity is still playing a great role in politics and industry. All over the world we now hear of voluntarism, privatization, decentralization, liberalization, deregulation etc. as countervailing policies to work against protectionism, monopoly and nationalization. A limit has to be put on the State taking upon itself the entire responsibilities for social welfare and growth. Managerial policies are naturally influenced by the state of affairs in a country depending on the degree of democratization and liberalization of the institutions and policies. Apart from the effect of the trade imbalance or deficit (which seems to be largely deciding government's policies and investment) on the nature of managerial expertise that is thrown up to meet the challenges, stimulating economic growth should be the prime criterion in bringing about changes in the policies. This growth is dependent on the progress of technology which may loosely be defined as making things trouble free or making them better and easier. Thus, there is an interplay of State policies and technologies which would influence the human resources development also.

Taking the case of Japan, which is leading the developed world, we have many lessons to learn. They are making marvelous strides which are viewed as miracles in every field. Their latest Facsimile machine is a giant leap in communication technology. The Japanese had only volcanos, salt water, sands, earthquakes and a nuclear holocaust. What is the secret for their globalization and leadership? "The incredible Japanese" by Parkinson (and others) gives some insight. It is mostly the commitment of the people for the cause of progress for common benefit. One can give a jocular equation too illustrate the point; 1 Indian=3 Japanese; 2 Indians=2 Japanese, 3 Indians=1 Japanese. That is how we are crushing the talent as we grow in numbers! The lesson is that we should provide the motivation and a sense of belonging to our people. This would be possible if merit is given encouragement at every level and not suppressed by extraneous considerations. In India we are losing sight of our eyes of 'learning and dedication to duty' and are preoccupied with selfishness and pettiness. Sacrifice is a forgotten virtue. Every individual should commit himself to the basic value of supporting the good and meritorious persons ignoring all other considerations of relationship, caste, creed, language, religion, colour etc., and we will achieve the miracle ourselves as the Japanese have done.

Tradition so-called is a deadly drag. It retards innovation and creativity. In India we are bogged down heavily by the wrong notions and values given to tradition in every walk of life. It is time we disabuse ourselves of the traditional myths and vain-glorious assertions of ancient greatness. We should open our eyes to the realities of the modern world and accept advanced ideas without reservations. It is taking years for us to adopt the financing techniques and services. When new technologies are breathing down our necks we still think in terms of counting of Beads and Homams for success. Why is our R& D so poor that for everything, even for making bricks, we have to import know-how? A good manager is one who is the best learner in a team. We have to impart vision, excitement, experimentation and freedom into our working.

Our communication philosophy is also primitive as we believe in personal attendance by people concerned instead of telecom methods. Treating it as a status symbol we deny the facility itself. Even a senior officer cannot use STD facility which is reserved to the topmost few! A retrograde system curtails communication. We are uncertain and suspicious in our working. Therefore, it is necessary to create a feeling of real stake in the welfare of the organization and provide participative management at all levels, so that an integration is achieved laterally and also vertically. Redoubling of effort may take place when we are in trouble. But this is not the proper way to derive satisfaction. The crisis management should be discouraged as much as the traditional junk management devoid of openness, which can produce only thumbless Ekalavyas and not Arjunas.

Productivity is ultimately through people. In other words, the human approach alone decides the success of an enterprise. Too much stress on procedures and streamlining may lead to what is called "analysis paralysis". We have become notorious for red tape bureaucracy. People should be inspired towards national commitment and excellence. This requires the creation of a climate of trust, openness and reciprocal as also general courtesy. Beyond the control and maintenance orientation which is traditional, our personnel policy should be development oriented. Maniacs, manipulators, bullies and unfriendly elements should be curbed. In certain conditions, these are the most successful people. To reverse this trend, opportunities should be created for merit to assert itself. Independence of opinion should be encouraged. Creativity and innovation should not be snubbed. Training methods are to be streamlined. Every assistance should be provided to enable the employees to work out their own development within and without the organization. Then only, we should be able to develop a management culture which would respond to the demands of the new situations in the highly competitive world that is emerging. Otherwise, we stagnate. No methods should be employed to create fear-psychosis or suspicion. Maternalistic attitudes will be rewarding. It is common knowledge that the noble mother bestows greater attention and care on the faltering child. This is not to say that discipline should be given up. It is to be developed in a human way with personalized attention wherever necessary. Howsoever highly placed, salves beget slavery. So, a good manager should free himself from haughtiness and indifference.

Every difference of opinion should not be taken as an affront or a challenge to authority. Sometimes, seeking information or clarification is taken as a confrontation, forgetting that there is education and mutuality in cooperation. This inferiority and power complex kills initiative. Teamwork is sometimes taken to mean groupism and a struggle towards opposite goals whereas it means the spirit of reaching excellence in the same direction. It is only when people recognize the relative merits of persons, provide competitive goals for their achievement and encourage their individuality and creativity they can attain the rightful place as an institution or as a nation. Spineless creeps who look downwards (feigning humility) for the crumbs of favours after retirement can not provide leadership as also those who act as hired henchmen. Eric Fromm, in his "Anatomy of human destructiveness" refers to these psychical cripples. Where has all our fabulous gold gone since we took to plastics, pin-cushions and paper-weights?

"Hope till hope creates from its own ruin, the thing it contemplates!"

Justice is not blind as usually depicted in the form of a blind woman with scales. Some people make a fetish of impersonal judgement as if they are born taskmasters. This will harden the sensibilities, damaging the spirit of belonging. An organization would be a living entity and reference to it as a family should be truly felt by one and all. We should encourage people to have self-respect. If a person has no respect for human dignity and goodness, he will operate at bottam levels of existence as he rises up in position. Flattery and imitation should be resisted. Discipline is not incompatible with dignity and self-respect and should not be identified with servility and personal attendance. Prejudice is not the same thing as opinion. The will to excel is a rare virtue. A good decision must have good reasons too. Competence is necessary for judgement and reasons are not to be invented. Where kindness is not possible impartiality is a must. III-treatment is not a method of management. A person who has no sympathy, patience or restraint should not be entrusted with power. The resolve to do good and selflessness act as the two hands of power in a worthy person. Unless superiors are properly educated in the above discussed values, the one-sided confidential and narrow-minded reports they may give can ruin the otherwise meritorious and bright careers.

Organisation with haughty and maladjusted managers and administrators may still progress: But, this is misleading. On close analysis, their success is seen to be due to routine and fortuitous factors. The final lesson to be learnt is that tenderness is the secret of real growth. Even the strongest oak puts forth the tenderest sprouts on its top.

See how tender is the eye
The same is true of the heart
The tongue and senses are tender
O Man, thy soul lies in tenderness!

– *Muchimilli*

Destructive propensities, abstention from work and cessation or closure of productive activity betray lack of commitment to national progress. In the pre-Independence days, such vandalism was probably an expression of anger of a helpless and suppressed people. It is a sad and shocking commentary or our education and social awareness when we find students, workers and others resorting to violence and destruction of public property running to crores of rupees at the slightest provocation. Freedom of collective bargaining or other trade union rights should not be misunderstood to be a licence to destroy the nation's wealth in any form whatsoever. Even strikes and lockouts are thus an anachronism in self-governing and developing country. Differences and protest can be expressed or channelised through responsible forums with out resulting in stoppage of work or destruction of property. Otherwise, the loss of time involved in recreating the wealth or recouping the losses is invaluable. Most of the industrialists and businessmen indulge in secreting the profits and wasting them on idle luxuries. They show little or no concern for the amenities to the workers and the pollution which is created all around by the neglect and parsimonious measures in the upkeep of the working places. The pollution of air, water and environment is avoidable if they sacrifice a little of their profits. This calls for a total reorientation in our systems and values.

Maternalistic management and humanistic economics will provide the answer for the present malaise of inadequate productivity and misplaced effort. Compulsory self-analysis or introspection as prescribed by the ancient seers, will mitigate the greed, power mania, self-aggrandisement, one-up-manship and other evil tendencies. A radical restructuring of our time and work schedules as different from slavish adherence to pre-independence systems, procedures and lifestyles will bring about the desired transformation. For example, in the educational institutions, besides revising the contents of the syllabus and textbooks to give them Indian orientation, students should be involved In social and field work. Minimum technical and physical training should be compulsorily imparted. There should be balance between formal and informal education throughout the career. This concept can be extended to the work in bureaucratic institutions also wherever possible.

A good human being is a real nucleus for change. This consciousness should inform all social and public activities and functions. People are generally indifferent to certain basic norms of good behaviour and decency. A simple instance is the rampant and reckless smoking habit which is playing havoc with the lives of millions. Smoking in trains, buses, offices, restaurants, meetings and even in religions places goes unchecked. The minimum self-restraint in such matters will improve the quality of life immensely. Advertisers resort to unscrupulous methods and the public media are indirectly canvassing for such agencies by including smoking scense in all situations. The lobbying has spread its tentacles. Similarly, adulteration of food stuffs and marketing of substandard medicines and spurious goods are indulged in or sponsored by even the educated people at one point or other. They do not search their conscience at all and live like selfish animals, by spoiling the atmosphere. The Gita enjoins on the learned and the leaders to set example to others "Yadyadacharti sreshtah". This applies to managers as well.

The quality of humans has to be reckoned as the index for the real wealth of a country or institution. Governments have the responsibility to provide the necessary infrastructure and the incentives for the growth of positive and vibrant society committed to peaceful existence in the comity of nations. A nation's development is dependent on healthy institutions and systems sustaining freedom, competitiveness, justice, harmony and universality. Certain values have to be inculcated from the very childhood. In the ultimate analysis, all the glib talk of human Resources Development is futile unless the seed of national commitment is implanted in childhood itself. Most children live estranged and isolated from nature. At school they carry huge loads of books with irrelevant and purposeless information. Psychologically, this makes them indifferent. They become easy prey to the cheap glamour of films and flippant life. The sense of productive orientation and time value system which is natural to life gets damaged and distorted. Those who are born into comfort lead easy lives. For the vast majority of people life is like a mere sand clock. Many laws governing our society were promulgated when there were no independent national institutions or Corporate Philosophy. We are bogged down by outdated concepts and a labyrinth of confusing laws, cumbersome procedures and sluggish system. Continuing the plethora of penalty clauses in our laws is a disgrace to a free nation. Very little has been done to revise them to suit the urgent progressive industrial and social requirements. It is said that senile and self-centred bandicoots without vision and modern learning cannot bring about the much needed radical reform in the various law and systems. The World Bank has attributed our slow progress to the purposeless proliferation and overlapping of the institutions. Given the political will we do not lack the expertise to meet the challenges. It is time we opened our eyes to our needs. Fortunately, there are welcome winds of change and I see a new dawn on the horizon.

One is pained to look at the present day picture of our society. Our education has failed us. The so-called intellectuals have made no impact on the diehards who cling to blind superstition and sentimental bigotry. People who live and die in this land are indifferent to its noble heritage of human values. What is the reason and where does the solution lie? We must have the boldness to analyse and propagate the correct understanding. The noble purpose of human birth should not be wasted in pettiness and selfishness. No religion preaches greediness, wickedness or violence. All the scriptures and the religious teachers advocate kindness, love, duty, service and such other human values. Given the opportunity and relevant education a human being will try to know the truth and live peacefully. This will mitigate the fanatical farce and spiritual pollution.

Man is the measure of all things. Have we not changed all our living habits and started using modern appliances, cosmetics, suits, ties, shoes and other personal necessities? People living in jungles, caves or deserts grew long hair, beards, nails etc. for facial protection or other historical reasons. Facilities were not there for body care.

There is always freedom to dress according to one's liking or taste without offending decency. But then, people should not try to look different and separate as belonging to different groups in offices and public places throughout their life.

Some "Sadhus" and "Munis" go naked in the name of religion even when giving discourses and moving among masses. Do they become less saintly if they wear some cloth? The external apparel with huge glittering robes, cap etc. of some priests make them look like buffoons. Is this the meaning of religion? Even the declaring of a National Holiday is held in suspense till the last minute depending on the sighting of the moon by a particular person. The disposal of dead bodies is another area that needs drastic reform. Thousands of acres of valuable land is turned into graveyards even when electric crematoria are available. We also make a huge farce with ashes of the dead persons. The sacred and personal sentiment is different from the sanctimonious public ceremonies, prolonged mourning etc., adding to the idleness and national loss already suffered. When millions are living in sub-human conditions is there any sense in this show of lavishness in the name of religious ceremonies? Are the educated people no more than escapists, conformists, cowards, sycophants, hypocrites and sanctimonious humbugs?

It is, therefore, imperative that we should analyse and evaluate some of the tenets in the modern context as a free nation, with openness, harmony and individual liberty as the guiding principles. The enduring principles of love, brotherhood, mutual help and sharing of the common heritage from time immemorial should give us the courage and conviction individually to overcome blind superstition sentimental and cumbersome prejudices, notions, practices etc. Every attempt should be made to promote the feeling of freedom and harmony internally and externally, in matters of dress, manners, behaviour, addresses, greetings etc. of the people so that we enjoy full freedom and live in peace and happiness as a well-knit and progressive family. We are not a spastic nation.

It's a pity that we are compelling our children to wear the fanatical symbols and appearances from childhood itself denying them the opportunity to develop free thinking ability. Teach them the noble tenets and hymns. Don't deny them the freedom to enjoy the fantasy, imagination, innocent playfulness, inquistiveness etc. which are the privileges of all children. It is cruel to force them to wear religious symbols, knotted hair, caps, pins etc. or other inconvenient appendages and to read or worship only a particular book or form as the one and the only representation of the Supreme. An image or symbol should give or represent freedom, inspiration, enlightenment, endearment, relief and liberation. Let them choose and taste the sweetness of the different sweets in the sweet shop!

Otherwise, we will harden the sensibilities, cripple the psyche and kill the spiritual freedom of the people, making them cowards and fanatics.

Are we not living by the food grown out of this land?
Are we not going to become part of its very soil and dust?
So, let's imbibe and preserve its great culture, good as gold
And make our children learn to feel proud of it, as we must;
We shall however, keep our windows widely open
For science and Technology and other healthy winds to blow in

To brighten our lives, removing poverty, illiteracy and suffering;
But we shall not be uprooted, if you care to know the meaning.
Rama and Ramcharit are our loftiest and thrilling tradition
Like the Himalayas and the Ganges, a perennial inspiration,
Their purity and life-giving messages
Are relevant to our modern situation
For preventing fissiparous tendencies
And for promoting National Integration.

The nation needs intellect, courage, uprightness and sacrifice which are on the decline. Appeasement, compromise, manipulation and greediness are on the increase. Respect for learning which has always been a unifying force has became a casualty in the rat-race for positions. The greatest need is to restore to "Learning" the place of eminence in all walks of life. The absurd fads, wretched astrological predictions by parasites and idlers, irrational beliefs in omens, mascots, inauspicious time, horoscopes, palmistry, numerology etc. are ruining our people robbing them of enterprise and faith in themselves or the Supreme. The charlatans, astrologers, tantrics and tricksters are exploiting the stupid and weak-minded people.

We have to radically change our parochial systems. The States are perpetrating the differences in language and religion. Besides, even in administrative matters regional disparities are accentuated. To give a simple example, a motor vehicle owner has to face nerve-racking harassment for re-registration etc. even if he is willing to pay the tax locally. Each State has its own peculiar rules in several areas of common interest like stamping, Registration, Sales tax, Duties etc. We are very very slow in changing our systems and methods for the better!

Even small nations have marched ahead of us. We looked for inspiration from abroad for our themes, projects, ideas and even slogans. The slave attitude had seeped into our way of life. A radical change was needed in our institutions, thinking and working. Are Marx and Mao more relevant to us than Gandhiji and Vivekananda! We should live up to the expectations of the Father of the Nation and march into the

21st Century holding our heads high and on our own shoulders as an integrated nation! In the conscious and subconscious levels we should feel that we are Indians first and last, forgetting our religious, regional, language, caste, creed, and other identities. We should prove to the world by our example that mankind is one large family and the barriers built by History and Wars can be obliterated by a common will for harmony and peace.

Prayer

This is my humble prayer to thee, my Lord,
That all men be healthy, happy and true,
And all women be graceful, loving and kind,
Proving the sweetness of home, ever and anew!

That all children learn the best lessons in schools
Which are modern with playgrounds, equipments and tools
And impart values and culture of national importance
Like Gandhian principles of harmony and self-reliance!

That young men be exposed to healthy habits and thoughts
And not to the depravity of films and literature of sorts;
They should feel the joy of service in their proud hearts
When alone can there be peace and progress in all parts!

That people believe in merit and sincere work for livelihood
Either in farms or factories or other places as good;
That every one from fanaticism and chicanery boldly dissent
And become Magnanimous, Action-oriented and Non-violent!

– *Muchimilli*

11

Ram Rajyam

A woman is synonymous with 'mother' in Hindu thought. That is the secret for the greatness! It takes deep analysis of the Vedic system in vogue in ancient India to appreciate the concept of motherhood as the fundamental value of women. The culmination was reached in the establishment of Ram Rajya, the heaven on Earth, where people lived in peace and prosperity. It can be said that Hinduism is unthinkable without Ram Rajya and vice versa. What is the use of philosophies and 'isms' if their practical results are inhuman societies? The pinnacle of Hinduism was the realisation of the purpose of life and creation on this Earth. It has deteriorated in time as a natural phenomenon and we see the misery and sufferings of people world-over. It is certainly possible to recreate, reform, regenerate and realise the practical dream of Ram Rajya. This was Gandhiji's life effort and goal for India. I have outlined the blue-print in this as part of Hinduism.

Preface to the New Edition

Some truths brook repetetion! In fact it is necessary to restate and emphasise certain eternal values for the guidance of mankind. That was the sole occupation of the ancient Indian sages (rishis). I was fortunate to have been born into a family of saints, mystics and poets. I was brought up in that tradition. I laboured to continue the heritage and rummaged the knowledge hills! In this edition, Ramrajyam is the chapter added in the end to reiterate the Gandhian outlook and understanding of Hinduism. Patience is always rewarded. It is particularly true in the field of learning. I have succeeded if I have brought out the gems from the ocean of Hinduism!

Ram Rajya: Ramayana's Uttarkand

After the long exile and the killing of demon Ravana, recorded in the epic Ramayana as Rama – Ravana war, Lord Rama along with Sitadevi, Hanuman, Lakshman and other friends arrived in Ayodhya. All of them were accorded a befitting and grand welcome and the whole world rejoiced on Ram's arrival after a long gap. This part of the epic Ramayana is known as Uttarkand.

In due course, Ram paid attention to the welfare of his kingdom and took control of the governance. His wish was to establish and turn his country into a place where the comforts, safety, friendship and well-being of each and every individual was paramount and, in the era, without parallel. This state of affairs is known as Ram Rajya.

Let us now analyse the yardstick Lord Ram set-up for Himself and to his people:

(a) The first and foremost of the guidelines was ensuring faith by him in his people and by his people in Him. Ram felt that without trust and faith, nothing can be achieved.

(b) The second was the governance of his vast empire. He divided his kingdom into small states and entrusted the duty of governing them to efficient and able colleagues with the responsibility of managing the affairs of their territories. They were given complete freedom to manage the day-to-day affairs of their domains.

(c) The Third was the rules to be followed by the rulers uniformly throughtout his country. All decisions were taken after taking into account all the aspects concerning the issue without favour or prejudice.

(d) The Fourth was the establishment of respect between the rulers and the people. There was no restriction for meeting the king by any person to get justice to his grievance anytime of the day or night. By this Ram wanted that his people should feel that they are important and justice is guaranteed to their problems without any delay.

(e) The Fifth was the establishment of brother-hood amongst his people and all of them respected and helped each other in need. By this Ram ensured that all are equal and helpful. Houses were kept open as there were no thefts. This was briefly the atmosphere of Ram Rajya during the Ramayan era and one now wonders if such a period will ever come to this great country called Bharat.

Ram Rajya or Welfare State

In India Ram Rajya is associated with the rule of Raja Rama chandra of Ayodhya the description of which is given in the Ramayana of poet Valmiki.

It is said of Ram Rajya that during that period none suffered from financial, mental or spiritual agony. In other words, it was the golden age of happiness, health, prosperity and perfection. In short, it was the model welfare state. It cared more for its people than for the State as an institution. This is why the people remember Raja Ram even today because Ram was a ruler who did not think of his benefits but of his people's welfare. These days the concept of Ram Rajya has become all the more significant and meaningful because people suffer a great deal at the hands of their State and its functionaries. In this age of ours there is nothing but selfishness, greed, materialism and obscenity. The subject has become a victim of poverty, unemployment, disease, starvation etc. and has no happiness, no peace of mind, no freedom of any sort. The present era in fact is the iron age with all its mechanical inventions and their adverse reactions. All things are State-controlled. The State is like a demon which devours its own children. The statesmen are no better that corrupt politicians. Bureaucracy has proved itself a necessary evil which interferes with all organizations, all plans of development and all forms of growth and progress. The industrialists are the real rulers who manipulate the affairs of the State to their advantage. The State has thus become an instrument to look after their interests at the cost of the miserable masses whose basic needs in life are totally neglected by all agencies. Under these circumstances the relevance of Ram Rajya is immanent because it alone can deliver the poor folk from the pangs of starvation, injustice, exploitation, crime and other countless miseries and abuses.

Ram Rajya is a very old concept, which is found in the legendary literatures of the world. Though Valmiki Ramayan defined it in Sanskrit in India, it was equally described in Hebrew in the old Testament in which the saints give pictures of the happy land of the God. Plato had painted a picture in his Republic, which creates an ideal Common Wealth with philosopher kings, community of gods and negation of private properties, for the happiness of citizens.

The ideal of a welfare state thus comes quite close to Sarvodaya preached by Mahatma Gandhi and Vinoba Bhave. In their scheme Sarvodaya is nothing but the modern version of the mythical Ram Rajya or Golden Era. These are all the accounts of ideal societies in which men lived as if they were gods with their hearts free from all sorrows. They are all pictures of Ram Rajya or ideal state where people live freely without care, sweat and worry, a life of endless joy and bliss.

In fact Ram Rajya is the concept of the State, the sole purpose of whose existence is to cater to the needs of its people. All States, which embrace socialism as their economical and political creed are such Ram Rajyas. Freedom-fighters, seers like Mahatma Gandhi, Vinoba Bhave, Jawaharlal Nehru and such other eminent Indians wanted to make India such a State. Ram Rajya ensured its people two fundamental principles: individuality and development.

In the ideal state there will be mutual help and co-operation for the development of the society as a whole, while the individual liberty is unfettered and unrestrained without any exploitation, crime and violence. Truth, justice and peace reign supreme. The rulers are to function as the servants of the people. Can we achieve this in the present political scenario where the people are divided on the lines of religion, caste, language etc! The welfare of majority people in India, for whom 'RAM' is 'marga darshak' in their day-to-day life, is the right path and it will pave the way for the creation of 'Ram Rajya' or welfare state of the modern times.

All educated people should work towards this noble cause and become worthy children of Mother India.

Ram Rajyam Prayer

The surest way to promote honest, purposeful and disciplined life with national feeling and human consideration. It may be made compulsory in all institutions, assemblies, schools etc. both public and private, to be daily read by one and all.

Personal

Strengthen me, Oh Lord! in my resolve to lead
A truthful life in thought, word and deed
And a purposeful life of sacrifice and service
To the poor and needy in their hours of crisis.

National

May I be helpful in building up the nation
Into an upright and hard-working civilization
Wasting no time.in idle pleasurers or ostentation
Till every Indian is free from fear of starvation.

International

May I truly feel the oneness with all human beings
And never cause them harm by my words or doings
May I strive to promote goodwill and tolerance
Which is the only way to individual and world peace.

PEACE PLEDGE

I shall work for peace by promoting cheerfulness and tolerance in thought, word and deed. I shall not get angry or use violence in any situation, public or private. "Respect for learning, Peace and Dedication to duty shall be my guiding principles.

PEACE PRAYER

O Lord! Your are all-pervading and living in all the beings throughout the world. Bless us to be aware of Thy presence in greater measure. Help us in our work for better and healthier life on this Earth. May there be peace and goodwill amongst all individuals and nations. This is my earnest prayer!

SANTI BABA'S PLEDGE

Every able person shall work for the peace and happiness of all and good of the society, and it shall ever be my endeavour to make every person so determined, if not so able! My life and skills shall become the instruments of peace.

12

Globalisation

The Hindu Sages believed in globalisation of knowledge ages ago in their utterances. It is now possible to realise their dream by the High-tech print media. We summarise the glorious thoughts in this short essay using the Alphabets as steps to convey them.

Acknowledge your debt to the Almighty for all the advantages you have over lakhs of people. Appropriate utilisation helps further evolution. (ii) Actions are right or wrong according as they promote union or separateness. (iii) Almost all ills and ailments are attributable to absence of love and affection in modern life.

Be bold to be objective and instrumental In benefitting the best in public life in thought, word and deed. Belittling the bright is baneful. Slaves beget slavery! Originality is oriental and ostentation is occidental.

Care and concern for children's growth and character is the crying need. Science and Technology with practical equipment must cover 90% of school curriculum. The colonial palaces must be converted to relieve the misery of our convents and colleges. Childhood is the formula for Nationhood!

Desire with your whole heart to leave the world a better place on your demise; You are divine. Selfish scheming is a scourge; Sacrifice is the ultimate gain. Overcome delusion which is threefold, viz. seeking: (1) selfish happiness; (2) faults in others and (3) physical permanence.

Every religion has enduring values and native relevance. Loving your Mother and Motherland above castes, creeds, faiths, etc. is the highest religion. Helping the poor likewise is the noblest.

Feel the true fame of fulfilment in your dutiful heart. Don't favour sycophancy and wasteful fanfare. Fabulous funds frittered away for false prestiges must flow into faculties, farms and factories.

Greatness is a quality different from grossness. One may not be the Sun; one can certainly be a candle. Gandhi grieved at the growth of self-aggrandisement and greed in rulers. Wearing Gandhi-cap alone is not enough!.

Gita is a giant step in the gamut of great Hindu Scriptures and Santi yoga is the path to the pinnacle of peace.

Honesty, hard-work and high ideals are hall-marks of leaders. Help them grow when you have the choice or means. Heaven has no bandicoots! Politics is not 'blind leading the blind' !

Irrigation to the land is what education is to the mind. India importing its food sounds illogical. Idle hands + waste lands = Golden fields. (ii) Flood the country with illustrated books on Nature, Science and Industry.

Juveniles are the hope of the Nation. The National Flag flies with their pride and purity. Protect them from pernicious pictures, habits and publications. Expose them to National needs, ideals and examples.

Kindness alone conquers. Others are only expedients. If the heart fails, the hand is of no avail. Managers are not savages! True power is like the fruit without thorns. The fruit lives; the thorns perish.

Languages are for convenience of communication and not for quarrels. Ennoble them like Sanskrit and appreciate their technical value. Discourage debasing lyrics and writings which are destroying our morals. Literature and Art must lend meaning to life. Laws and Rules are levers for removing the stumbling-blocks.

Man is the highest form of evolution in the scheme of creation. We must prove worthy of our endowments and eradicate sub-human conditions. Even a little thought counts greatly in this regard. Minimise meaningless pursuits and paraphernalia not related to public good.

Nature provides nourishment and equality to Man. We should show our gratitude by nourishing nature. Ecology needs eternal vigilance! Sanitation is civilisation !

Opportunities for doing good offer them-selves to every person. The strength of character decides the course of action.

Prosperity means progress of science and technology of a peace-loving people. Warmongers work for the wreck forgetting the oneness of Mankind.

Quintessence is a hallowed word. It implies "Essentialism" which is conducive to the happiness of man and good of the society. All knowledge must subserve these twin objectives.

Reason and rationality should inform social and religious institutions also. Superstition, Fatalism and Fanaticism are mental parasites. Encourage science and spirituality.

Spiritualism is the sublimation of enlightened self-interest. Beware of simpletons and sinners masquerading as prophets and priests. Mercenaries cannot be mentors. Saint-hood is universal. Service is spirituality.

Thoughts motivate action. Healthy, nation--building and work-oriented ideas must be implanted from childhood. Science and Service should replace History and Luxury.

Universe and Atom have ceased to be unfathomable. But Man has become uncontrollable, meaning destruction and devastation, contrary to all commandments and counsels (e. g. 'Do not kill'-but prepare (w) hell !)

Value your time. Waste it not in witnessing crime and vulgarity. Veer the people around you as Votaries of work and not vices. Verily, the truest joys in life flow from diligent discharge of our destined duties.

Wonder like a child at the manifestation of the Supreme in and around you. A wealth of joy awaits you always. Awaken others to this awareness!

XYZs or alibis and fads shall not bother or bamboozle you. You have the wisdom of the Lord already seated in your heart which is ever wakeful. Trust its voice and do the right.

Bibliography

History of Dharma Sastra by Pandurang Vaman Kane
Rig Veda Samhita by H.H. Wilson
The Dharma Sastra or the Hindu Law Codes Ed. By M.N. Dutt
The Yazur Veda Samhita by Ralph T.G. Griffith
Atharva Veda Samhita by William Dwight Whiteny
The Sama Veda by Devichand
Encyclopedia of Puranic beliefs and practices by Sadashiv A. Dange
India - Mother of us all, Ed. Chaman Lal
Brahma Sutras by Vimalanada Bharati, Courtallam
The Koran by E.H. Palmer (The World's classics)
Ramacharitmanas by Gita Press, Gorakpur
Yajur Veda by Gita Press, Gorakpur
Rig Veda by Charla Ganapati Sastri, Visakhapatnam
Atharva Veda by John Muir
Vedanta Sutras (Sacred Books of the East) by George Thibaut
The Dance of Shiva by Ananda Coomaraswamy
Sacred books of the East Ed. Max Mueller
Bhagavatgita by Gita Press
Regveda Samhita
Yajurveda Samhita
The Upanishads

Brahma Sutras

Srimad Bhagavatam

Ramayana of Valmiki

Maha Bharata of Vyasa

Viveka Chudamani of Sankara

The Dhammapada

The Gospel of Sri Ramakrishna by M.

Philosophies of India, Ed. Joseph Campbell

Samkya Karika by Colebrooke and Wilson

Yoga Sutra of Patanjali

Viseshika Sutras of Kanada by A.E. Gough,

Upanishads by Swami Sharvananda

The Philosophy of Visishtadvaita by P.N. Srinivasachari

Purnaprajna by Darsana S. Subha Rau

Jainism by Hermann Jacobi

Buddhism by H.C. Warren

The Spiritual heritage of Tyagaraja, Sri Ramakrishna Math, Madras

Nibbana – Narada Maha Thera

The Golden Rules of Buddhism by H.S. Olcott

Tattvaloka (The Splendour of Truth) by Sringeri Mutt Vo. XV No. 1

Peace by Sri Santi Ashram-Vol. XIX

Sapthagiri by Tirumala Tirupati Devastanam – Vol. XXII (TTD)

Friedrich Nietzsche by Maximilian A. Mugge

Vedic Mathematics by Sri Bharati Krishna Tirthaji Maharaja

Glimpses of World History by Jawaharlal Nehru

Hindu Civilization by Radha Kumud Mookerji

The Indus Civilization by Earnest Mackay

The Rig-Veda by Kaegi (Translates by R. Arrowsmith)

The Oxford History of India by Vincent A. Smith

The Thirteen Principal Upanishads translated by R.E. Hume

A History of Civilization in Ancient India by Romesh Chunder Dutt

A History of Sanskrit literature by A.A. Macdonell

The Early History of India by Vincent A. Smith

Kautilya's Arthasastra translated by R. Shamasastry

Buddhist India by T.W. Rhys Davids

An Advanced History of India by R.C. Mazumdar

The Song Celestial by Edwin Arnold

The Light of Asia by Edwin Arnold

The Ramayana and Mahabharata by Romesh Chunder Dutt

Bhagvad–Gita by L.D. Barnett

The Discovery of India by Jawaharlal Nehru

Indian Education in Ancient and Later Times by F.E. Keay

The Indus Civilization by Ernest Mackay

Mohenjo-daro and the Indus Civilization by Sir John Marshall

The Wisdom of the Aryas by Bennett, Allan

Essays on religion and philosophy of the Hindus by H.T., Colebrooke

The Sarva Darsana Samgraha or Review of the Different Systems of Hindu Philosophy by E.B. Cowell and Cough, A.E.

A History of Indian Philosophy by S.N. Dasgupta

Encyclopaedia of religion and Ethics. By Hastins, James, ed.

Brahmanism and Hinduism by Monier-Williams

The Six Systems of Indian Philosophy by Mueller, Max

A Constructive Survey of Upanishadic Philosophy by Ranade, R.D.

The Aryan Ideal by T.L., Vaswani

The Complete works of Swami Vivekananda

The Aphorisms of the Nyaya philosophy of Gautama by J.R. Ballantyne, ed.

A History of Indian Logic; ancient, medieval, and modern schóols by Vidyabhasna, Satisachandra

The Vaisesika Sutras by Sinha, Nandalal

The Samkhya System by Keith, A. Berriedale

The Vedanta Doctrine of Sri Sankaracharya by Sastri A. Mahadeva

The Vedanta Sutras by Thibaut, George

The Serpent power by Avalon, Arthur

The Garland of Letters by Abinas Chandra Das

Indo-Aryans by Rajendralal Mitra

Hymns of the Atharva Veda Tr. M. Bloomfield. (Sacred Books of the East)

Everyday life in Ancient India by Padmini Sengupta

New Testament by the Gideons International

Thus spoke Jesus Christ by Anchor Books